MW01629313

COLLABORATIVE MARRIAGE SKILLS

COUPLE COMMUNICATION I

Sherod Miller, Ph.D.

Phyllis A. Miller, Ph.D.

Elam W. Nunnally, Ph.D.

Daniel B. Wackman, Ph.D.

Fifth Edition of COUPLE COMMUNICATION I
Second Printing, January 2010

**Interpersonal
Communication
Programs, Inc.**

**30772 Southview Dr.
Evergreen, CO 80439
Toll-Free: 800-328-5099**
www.couplecommunication.com

A Brief History of Couple Communication

The roots of COUPLE COMMUNICATION extend back to the University of Minnesota Family Study Center, where it was first developed and researched through the work of Sherod Miller, Elam Nunnally, and Daniel Wackman in the early 1970s. The team began Interpersonal Communication Programs, Inc. (ICP) to train instructors and distribute the program with the purpose of teaching couples how to become their own best problem solvers. This was a pioneering approach at the time. Through the structured course, couples learned communication maps, a specific set of talking and listening skills, and a conflict-resolving process.

From the beginning, ICP has encouraged independent research on its programs and applications of them. A large body of research exists on COUPLE COMMUNICATION, much of it done in the earlier years, which established its effectiveness. In fact, it is the most researched marriage-education program available. For a summary of the research, visit: www.couplecommunication.com, and click on research.

To date, more than 700,000 couples around the world have participated in COUPLE COMMUNICATION. The program has been translated into several languages. The authors have received four awards from national and international marriage and family organizations for their research and development of COUPLE COMMUNICATION.

Along the way, Phyllis Miller joined the team. ICP has continued to develop programs, including COUPLE COMMUNICATION II and programs for business and individuals.

This is the fifth edition of COUPLE COMMUNICATION I since its origination. As the others before it, this revision retains the research-supported basic skills that stand as the foundation of the program. Each revision has brought refinements to the frameworks, better learning methodology, and new features. This revision includes all of these things plus a conceptualization of collaborative marriage and the integration of new insights gained from the field of neuroscience.

Daniel Lord, Ph.D., Professor of Marriage and Family at Friends University, has contributed substantially to this edition and to the development of ThriveSphere: The Collaborative Marriage Inventory. Fred Jakolat, MA, and Roy Anderson, MA, Licensed Marriage & Family Therapist, both Certified COUPLE COMMUNICATION Instructors, have also influenced this revision. William Bailey, Ph.D., Professor of Marriage and Family at the University of Arkansas, facilitated the initial research of ThriveSphere questions.

COUPLE COMMUNICATION could never have had the impact it has achieved without the dedicated instructors who bring it to life. This revision owes so much to their valuable feedback and encouragement.

The Addition of Scripture

Over the years, many instructors have sent us scripture verses that relate to sections of the COUPLE COMMUNICATION program. From these suggestions and our own study, we have chosen the verses included in this edition. We offer them for your reflection, discussion, and prayer.

You can find the scripture verses on the back side of each chapter divider page. An exercise to apply scripture is located on the last page of each chapter.

The Collaborative Marriage Inventory

ThriveSphere is a self-partner-relationship awareness tool — a healthy relationship map — to help you and your partner build a collaborative marriage. Its set of questions yields a "reflectment" of your life together. The tool is:

- Accessible — lets you and your partner each take it online at your convenience.

- Quick and easy — takes you each 15 to 20 minutes to complete the questions.

- Comprehensive — covers the major aspects of your relationship based on the 7 dimensions of a collaborative marriage.

- Visual — displays your individual and couple responses to all the questions on a Sphere-Chart, a visual map.

- Insightful — shows your individual views of your relationship strengths, as well as areas you choose together to develop.

- Coordinated — captures your use (or lack of use) of the concepts, skills and processes taught in COUPLE COMMUNICATION.

- Low cost — allows you to take ThriveSphere three different times for one total price of the tool.

Your COUPLE COMMUNICATION Instructor guides you through a discussion of your Sphere-Chart.

Feedback is presented in a unique graphic format that enables you to view your relationship as a whole — as interrelated and interconnected parts. The tool helps you review, discuss, and focus your learning.

We encourage you to take ThriveSphere three times to record your growth:

1. Prior to taking COUPLE COMMUNICATION I
2. Sometime shortly after completing the program
3. Again, within 12 months , or after some time passes

Taking ThriveSphere is not a requirement to participate in COUPLE COMMUNICATION. However, our experience indicates you will gain more from the program if you do so.

TO TAKE THRIVESPHERE

Contact your COUPLE COMMUNICATION Instructor. He or she will provide you with the URL (web address) for you each to take ThriveSphere online, and schedule a time to meet with you to review your relationship map.

For more information about ThriveSphere, see **www.ThriveSphere.com**

Ground Rules and Course Materials

GOALS

The goals of COUPLE COMMUNICATION I are for you as a couple to:

- Improve your day-to-day communication.
- Make better decisions and resolve issues skillfully.
- Increase satisfaction in your relationship.

In other words — for you and your partner to create and sustain a collaborative marriage.

GROUND RULES

As you learn the skills and processes of this program, keep the following ground rules in mind:

- *Participate voluntarily* in any activity (exercise) or discussion. If for any reason you do not choose to participate, say so. You can pass.
- *Respect boundaries.* Every individual and couple has their own informational boundaries. Take your own and others' into account. To do this:

  1. Identify or choose issues you think are appropriate to talk about in this setting.

2. Do not pressure anyone else to disclose anything he or she does not wish to disclose.

■ *Choose real issues* as you focus on skill practice. It is best to start with smaller issues instead of major ones as you learn the skills and processes.

■ *Assume you will be coached* by the instructor and others in the class. Coaching and receiving feedback are essential for skill learning.

COURSE MATERIALS

As a couple, you need to have your own "Couple Packet," the materials you use as:

■ Guides for learning during the workshop

■ Aids for practice on skills between sessions

■ Application, reference, and reinforcement tools after the program is completed.

The Couple Packet includes:

■ Two COLLABORATIVE MARRIAGE SKILLS Workbooks

■ One Awareness Wheel Skills Mat

■ One Listening Cycle Skills Mat

■ Two Awareness Wheel Pads

■ Two set of Pocket Cards.

CONTENTS

Contents

7 Dimensions of a Collaborative Marriage

Collaboration is a very high way of relating.

In marriage, collaboration involves a strong man and a strong woman who can bridge to each other, committed to building a mutually satisfying and fulfilling relationship, across a lifetime together.

Collaboration is a choice for using — and responding to — the power of two individuals. It is not accommodating (just giving in to another) or dominating (forcing your way with another). Rather, the process accepts both partners as bringing qualities of importance and value to the relationship.

Drawing on one another's talents and experiences, a couple chooses a purposeful journey with each other that neither one of them could have created alone — the whole is greater than the sum of its parts. They employ "a collaborative operating system" in their relationship that gives them the ability to handle the challenges they face on the road before them. Over time, this way of being together also builds a reservoir of respect and appreciation for each other.

A collaborative marriage does not come naturally. It requires knowledge, skill, and attention, seasoned with love. COUPLE COMMUNICATION provides maps, skills, and processes — practical tools — that can help you build a collaborative marriage so that you and your partner can fulfill your hopes and dreams across your life together.

THE 7 DIMENSIONS

These relationship dynamics go into developing and sustaining a collaborative marriage:

1. *Committing* to Partnership
2. *Caring* Actively for Self, Partner, and Us
3. *Considering* Life's Concerns and Opportunities
4. *Communicating* with Skill to Connect
5. *Cooperating* to Resolve Issues
6. *Celebrating* Our Life Together
7. *Contributing* to Life Around Us

DESCRIPTIONS OF THE DIMENSIONS

1. *Committing* to Partnership

The word commitment scares many people, especially guys. Numerous jokes and phrases about getting married revolve around notions of being trapped, stuck, or captured. The underlying theme is loss — giving up freedom. Ironically, commitment brings the opposite — gaining freedom.

Commitment — the choice each of you makes for the partnership — provides the foundation for a collaborative marriage. It supplies mutual boundaries that surround the physical and psychological "relationship zone" unique to you as a couple. Commitment brings:

- Predictability in a sea of change.
- Trust and confidence that frees you to go about important things in life.
- Enjoyment of belonging and loyalty.
- The fruits of honesty and priority.
- Shared intimacies and confidences.
- A platform for pursuing your dreams and building an intentional future.

Your potential for a collaborative marriage increases when you share a common set of values and behaviors that support committing to each other for a lifetime together. As in any decision, with commitment, each of you gives up something to gain something. The task is to let go of any loss, and embrace the benefits, building on the advantages and potentials of your choice.

2. *Caring* Actively for Self, Partner, and Us

Every communication with your partner contains two component parts:

- *Behavior — the verbal and nonverbal actions you take — which stem from your underlying attitudes.*
- *Attitude — the mental view you hold — which comes from a combination of your beliefs, feelings, and intentions.*

The attitudes most important to your behavior revolve around caring or uncaring:

- Caring — valuing, respecting, or taking into account (counting)
- Uncaring — not valuing, not respecting, or not taking into account (not counting)

Either attitude represents your momentary or long-term assumptions about one another's significance.

Behavior Reflects Attitude

Your communication behavior, in an exchange with your partner, reflects one of the two basic attitudes you hold towards yourself:

- I Care About Me (a caring arrow up)
- I Don't Care About Me (an uncaring arrow down)

You express either that you value, respect, and count yourself — you care — or that you do not.

Partner:

Likewise, in communicating with your partner, your behavior displays one of two corresponding attitudes you hold towards him or her:

- I Care About You (a caring arrow up)
- I Don't Care About You (an uncaring arrow down)

You demonstrate either that you value, respect, and count your partner — you care — or that you do not.

- In a collaborative relationship, the gold standard is to live with both your own and your partner's arrows up — caring for us.

3. *Considering* Life's Concerns and Opportunities

The most loving relationship or rewarding intimacy does not erase life's complications. Even good things — like a new job or home, or the blessings of children — bring stress. Every couple encounters their own unique set of concerns and opportunities across time.

- These challenges become issues to be engaged constructively and managed as well as possible.
- The better a couple is at handling commonplace issues, the more robust and resilient their relationship.

THRIVE, the Collaborative Marriage Sphere, and information in Chapter 2 of this workbook, can guide you to a clearer picture of your issues. Every aspect of COUPLE COMMUNICATION is designed to increase your skill in responding to these everyday challenges of couple life. Your success in small things builds trust and confidence for your managing big challenges just as well.

4. *Communicating* with Skill to Connect

For thousands of years, many couples have been communicating with a caring spirit. No substitute exists for a loving and respectful attitude in an exchange. However, even with a genuinely caring attitude, communication can be unclear, inept, or misunderstood. This is where skill enters.

Behavioral scientists who study human communication have discovered that *certain behaviors yield more predictable outcomes.*

- Based on self-awareness, specific talking skills enable the sending of clear messages.
- Likewise, specific listening skills support accurate other-awareness and understanding.

Introduction

- Together these talking and listening skills help couples connect by the partners responding to each other's interests and needs more effectively and efficiently.

- These two skill sets are central to accomplishing that all-important sense of truly being heard, known, and understood by one another.

- Communication skills also play a big part in how well couples can repair and recover from the damage of inevitable and occasional offensive behaviors, broken promises, or unfulfilled expectations.

Behavior and Attitude in Combination

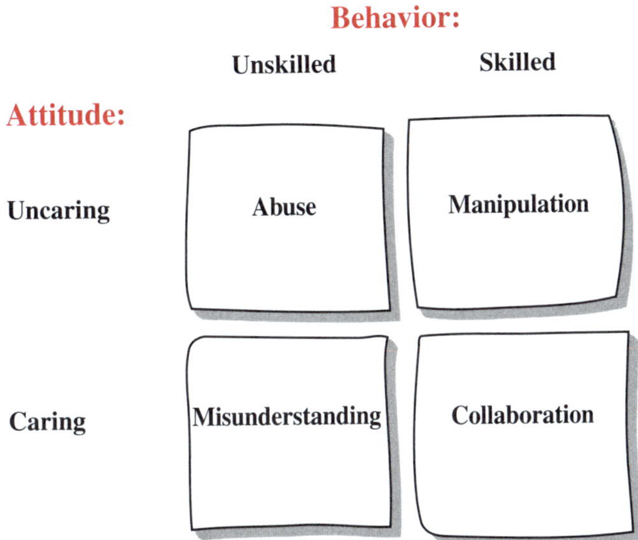

- An uncaring attitude and unskilled communication behavior, combined in a relationship, make for difficult living. The result can be some form of *abuse*, ranging from verbal to emotional, and even possibly, to physical abuse.

- Without a caring attitude, unfortunately, learning and using COUPLE COMMUNICATION skills can turn you into a more sophisticated *manipulator*. And if your partner discounts himself or herself and allows your manipulative behavior to continue, your relationship will suffer. Either uncaring attitude or unskilled communication behavior can retard, hurt, or destroy a relationship.

- Even with a caring attitude, the lack of skills can cause you and your partner to bump into regular *misunderstandings*.

- By combining a caring attitude and skills in communication, as a couple, you can connect with each other more positively, strengthen your relationship, and create a *collaborative* partnership. Chapters 3 and 4 in this workbook give you practical skills to add to a caring attitude.

5. *Cooperating* to Resolve Issues

The way you and your partner go about setting goals, making plans, negotiating decisions, or handling differences and conflicts influences the level of satisfaction that one or both of you feel about your relationship. In facing all of these activities of life, you can spin out and fail to cooperate in various ways, such as by avoiding or forcing decisions, to name two options.

A caring attitude and skilled communication give you reliable traction for heading into important issues that deserve your best cooperation. Being able to harness the power of collaborative conversations will allow you to be more productive and consistent when facing difficult-to-resolve issues. With practice, this also will help you anticipate and complete decision-making with greater confidence and less stress. The result can be more than a viable marriage; it can be a thriving one, as well. Chapter 5 in this workbook provides a plan — actually a map — for using your power of conversation to accomplish this important relationship quality.

6. *Celebrating* Our Life Together

Intimate friendship — companionship — is at the heart of collaborative marriage. Your relationship grows simply by your being together — whether in silence, in conversation, or in doing an activity — enjoying each other's presence. Celebrating your togetherness plays out in many ways:

- Small, fun, private humorous exchanges.

- Affectionate knowing looks.

- Appreciative comments.

- Regular or occasional small rituals — having coffee together, taking short walks, etc. — as well as special celebrations — anniversaries, birthdays.

- Looking forward to seeing each other at the end of a day or after you have been apart longer.

- Speaking words of endearment to each other that express your special love.

Spending a lifetime together creates a unique and privately shared history — through tough and pleasant times — that is known, savored, and celebrated primarily by the two of you. It is your world, a landscape you have traveled, explored, and changed through your relationship together. Being proactive in celebrating your own bond lessens the impact of life's stress and boosts your health-promoting energy at the same time.

7. *Contributing* to Life Around Us

A collaborative marriage is not an end in itself. It goes beyond self and partnership to serving and helping others. Giving beyond the usual circle of concerns expands horizons and changes perspective of life itself. As two individuals sharing a couple-life together, contributing extends from:

- Giving birth to, adopting, raising and positioning children to live their own successful lives.
- Caring for parents, friends, neighbors, or others in dependent situations.
- Sharing time and money for needs in a local community or in the wider world.

A genuinely collaborative marriage develops its own special sense of purpose, mission, and meaning that brings more to the planet than it takes and consumes. Fulfilling this mission and meaning brings a deep sense of reward shared by the two of you who have claimed and pursued it. The skills you learn in COUPLE COMMUNICATION reach their most lasting imprint on your life as you use them for this special purpose.

> If the ax is dull and its edge unsharpened, more strength is needed but skill will bring success. *Ecclesiastes 10:10*

CARING ABOUT SELF AND PARTNER

Instructions: Use the space below to list the different ways you demonstrate caring for yourself and your partner.

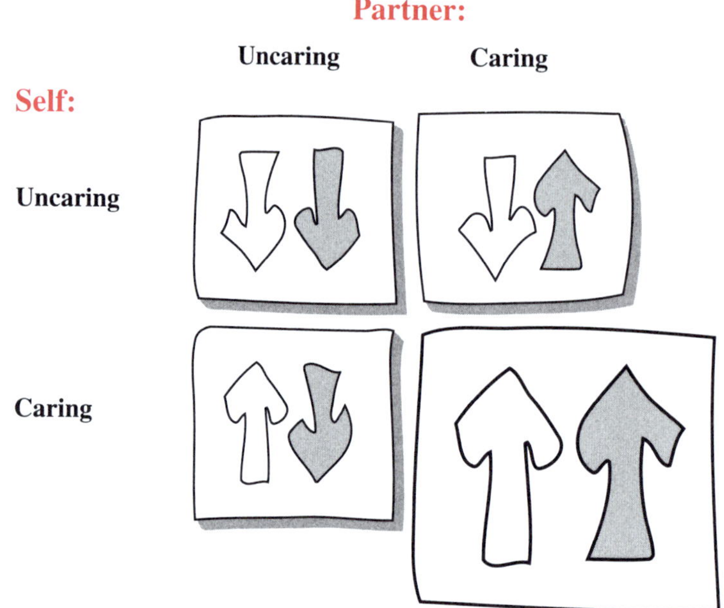

Caring for yourself:

Caring for partner:

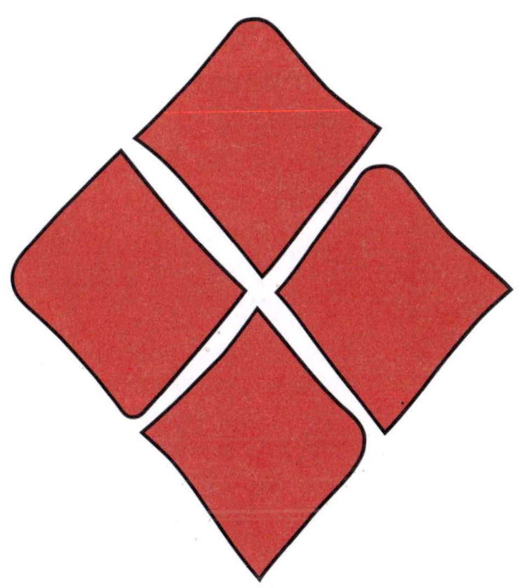

CHAPTER 1

Scripture for Choosing Styles of Communication

Consider the following scriptures as they relate to styles of communication — particularly in reference to the way you talk to your partner:

The tongue that brings healing is a tree of life, but a deceitful tongue crushes the spirit. *Proverbs 15:4*

A word fitly spoken is like apples of gold in settings of silver. *Proverbs 25:11*

Pleasant words are a honeycomb, sweet to the soul and healing to the bones. *Proverbs 16:24*

Do not let any unwholesome talk come out of your mouth, but only what is helpful for building others up according to their needs that it may benefit those who listen. *Ephesians 4:29*

Do not repay evil with evil or insult with insult, but with blessing, because to this you were called so that you may inherit a blessing. Whoever would love life and see good days must keep his tongue from evil and his lips from deceitful speech. *1 Peter 3:9 and 10*

Drive out the mocker, and out goes strife; quarrels and insults are ended. *Proverbs 22:10*

Words from a wise man's mouth are gracious, but a fool is consumed by his own lips. *Ecclesiastes 10:12*

A gentle answer turns away wrath, but a harsh word stirs up anger. *Proverbs 15:1*

Let your conversation be always full of grace, seasoned with salt, so that you may know how to answer everyone. *Colossians 4:6*

But I tell you that men will have to give account on the day of judgment for every careless word they have spoken. For by your words you will be acquitted, and by your words you will be condemned. *Matthew 12: 36-37*

1

CHOOSING COMMUNICATION STYLES

Communication Styles Map
Styles of Talking
The "Low Road" and the "High Road"

Whether you are talking with your partner or with someone else, each time you say something, your message contains two parts:

- *What* you say — the content
- *How* you say it — the style

What you talk about makes a difference, yet your style — *how* you talk about something — has the greatest impact on your communication. Your verbal and nonverbal style is a command or relational message. It tells others the way to take your message about the content — whether you are joking, angry, tentative, or serious. It also conveys a caring or uncaring attitude.

Likewise, you can vary your style of listening. How you listen has a measurable effect on the quality of information the other person shares.

Since people respond to *how* as much as they do to *what*, the outcome of a conversation can vary considerably depending on the talking and listening styles you use in the process. Your style either helps or interferes with your ability to connect and communicate effectively.

Many "failures to communicate" stem from using an ineffective style of communication for the situation.

COMMUNICATION STYLES MAP

How you talk and listen to someone falls into one of four major communication styles, shown in the map below:

- Each of the talking styles corresponds to a listening style.

- Every style has typical behaviors — unskilled or skilled — associated with it that have a highly predictable impact upon a conversation.

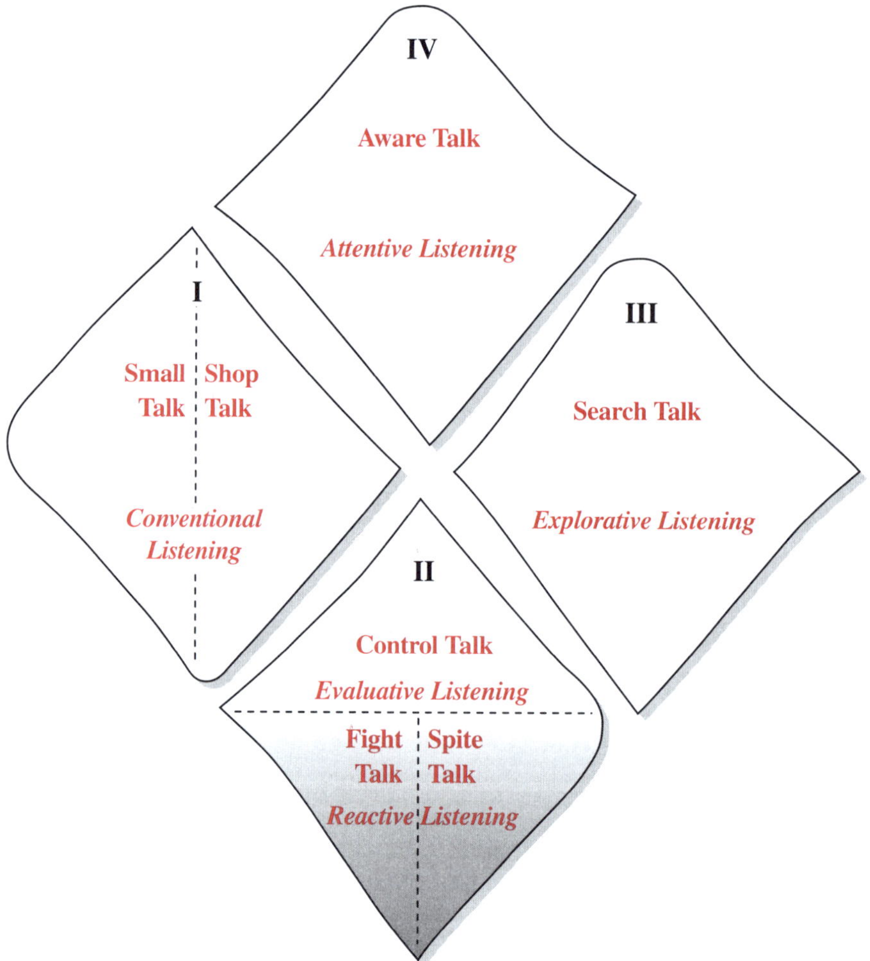

This chapter focuses on talking, the sending side of a conversation. Chapter 4 presents styles of listening, the receiving side of communication.

STYLES OF TALKING

STYLE I — Small Talk and Shop Talk

Small Talk and Shop Talk are the pleasant ways couples use to connect and to exchange routine information.

SMALL TALK

Small Talk is the light conversation or chit chat about everyday things. It ranges from cordial and friendly to sharing little intimacies. While this way of talking may be commonplace, it is exceptionally important for staying connected and confident with each other.

Intention to:
connect
update
enjoy each other
maintain harmony
stay in touch

Intention to be:
friendly
pleasant
sociable
playful
available

Mood
relaxed
contented
calm
comfortable
peaceful

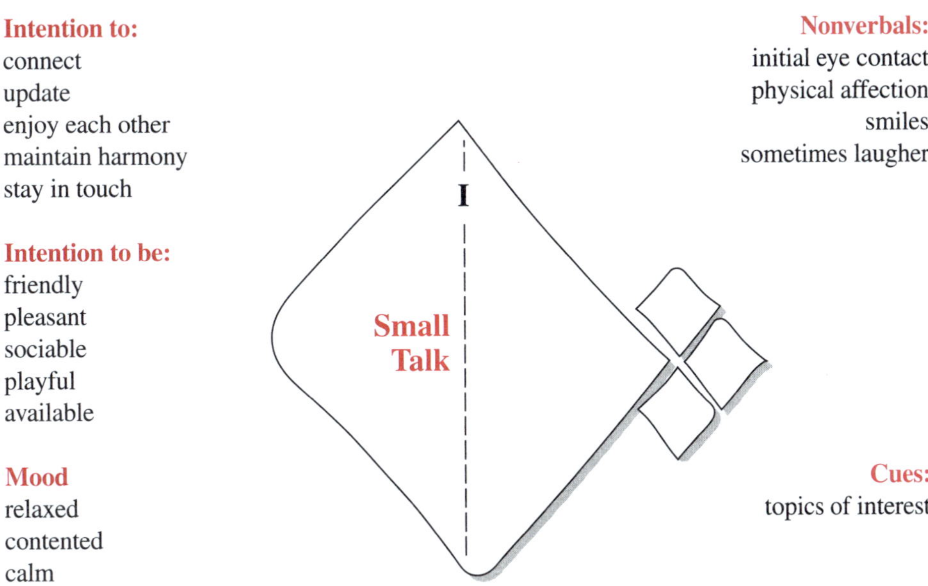

This style:

- Facilitates comfortable "comings" and "goings," connecting and disconnecting.
- Supplies an initial sense (visual and tonal) of how well each partner is doing.
- Allows each person to synchronize, "get up to speed," with the other by reliving the day's activities, events, and challenges.

- Provides a way of simply being together, sharing activities, and enjoying each other.

- Can be used to cover, skirt, deflect, or avoid dealing with an unresolved issue.

- Lessens, (or disappears) when couples experience:

    Severe or continuous conflict.

    Extended pressures or stress, for example, from extensive work schedules.

Typical Small-Talk Behaviors

Greetings, hellos and goodbyes: "Hi, how are you doing?" "See you later."

Catching up: "What did you do today?"

Sharing experiences and events of the day: "You won't believe what happened at work this afternoon. I met with . . ."

Commenting on news, weather, sports: "Who do you think will win the election?"

Lighthearted, non-hostile joking: "You're not a very good influence on me."

Storytelling: "When I was growing up, my Dad would say . . . ."

Recalling or anticipating events: "Remember when we . . . " "I'm excited about our vacation plans."

Non-hostile joking: Private, inside relationship jokes that are fun for both partners

Impact of Small Talk

- Relaxes and refreshes a relationship.
- Sometimes lightens a tense mood and eases pressure.
- Keeps conversation on an ordinary, surface level.
- Fosters annoyance if the other person wants to go to a more serious or deeper level.

> Your Small Talk as a couple demonstrates that you are
> connecting with and enjoying one another.
> Without it, as time passes, you grow distant.

SHOP TALK

Shop Talk is the conversation about tasks and necessary details of living.

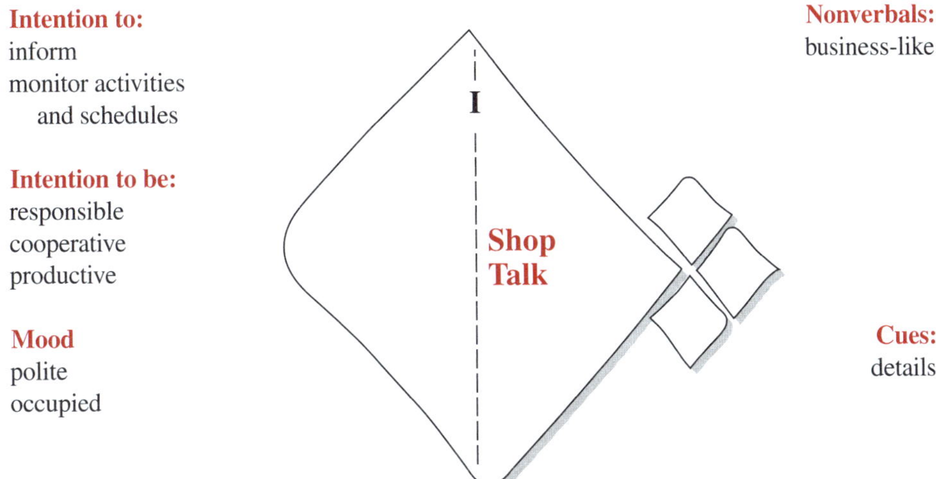

Typical Shop Talk Behaviors

Planning, scheduling: "The game starts at 1 pm today. We need to be there by 12:30."

Reporting facts, observations: "Susan's throat culture was negative, even though it looked red."

Taking initiative, checking up, following up: "Did we get our house tax statement yet?"

Coordinating, making routine decisions: "I decided to get the car greased and oiled today if that fits your plans for the day."

Impact of Shop Talk

- Handles routines or informs of changes in the maintenance of your life.

> Shop Talk keeps things moving and organized, but if that's all there is for you as a couple, your relationship lacks vitality.

STYLE II — Control, Fight, and Spite Talk

Through power and control, this style aims at gaining agreement or compliance, or it attempts to resist change. When using Style II, you strive for a certain outcome, even if it has to be forced. You focus on the other person — not yourself.

Partners try to exert their power using three different ways of talking in Style II. The first way — Control Talk — sends messages intended to be constructive. The other two — Fight Talk and Spite Talk — send negative, potentially destructive messages. Nonverbals — posture, gestures, tone, pitch, pace and facial expressions— play a prominent role in signaling these messages.

CONTROL TALK

Control Talk intends to take charge — communicating a knowing, authoritative stance. This is a style most people use to direct, command, make a presentation, persuade, sell, bargain, supervise, teach, and advocate.

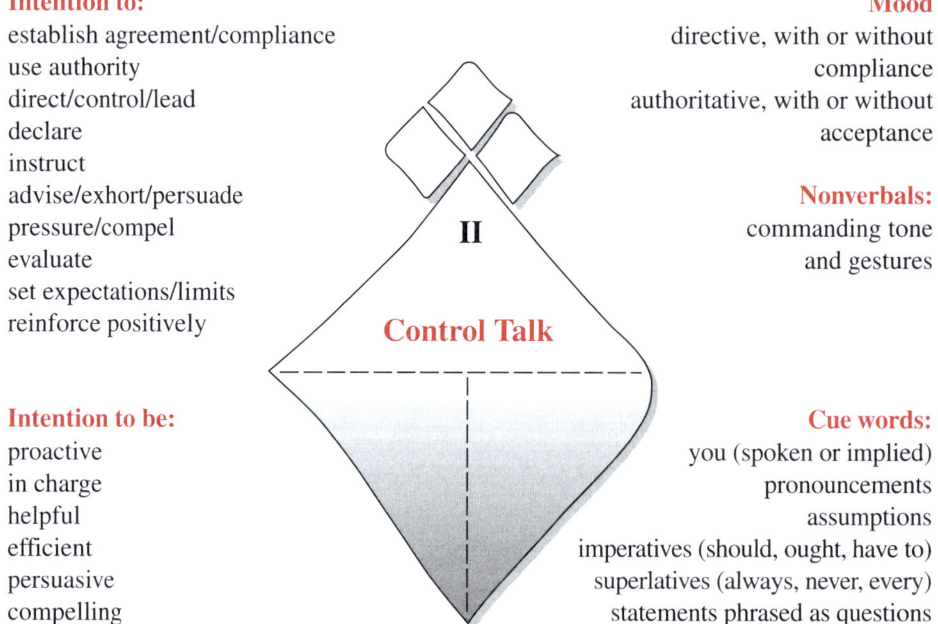

Intention to:
establish agreement/compliance
use authority
direct/control/lead
declare
instruct
advise/exhort/persuade
pressure/compel
evaluate
set expectations/limits
reinforce positively

Intention to be:
proactive
in charge
helpful
efficient
persuasive
compelling

Mood
directive, with or without compliance
authoritative, with or without acceptance

Nonverbals:
commanding tone and gestures

Cue words:
you (spoken or implied)
pronouncements
assumptions
imperatives (should, ought, have to)
superlatives (always, never, every)
statements phrased as questions

Typical Control-Talk Behaviors

Speaking for others — tell others what their experience has been, is, or will be: "You know this is the right decision."

Directing: "Stop by the cleaners on your way home."

Advising, prescribing solutions: "Take some vitamin C. It will help you ward off a cold."

Advocating, persuading: "Just try it once. You will really like it."

Instructing: "There are three things to consider. The first is . . . ."

Evaluating: "This new software is twice as good as the old program."

Assuming: "It isn't hard. You can figure it out."

Setting expectations, establishing boundaries: "Let's get together tomorrow afternoon, just the two of us."

Cautioning, warning: "Be careful. The roads are slick."

Closed/directive questions: "Don't you think that . . . ?" "Wouldn't you agree that . . . ?

Praising: "You look great in your new blue suit."

Bragging: "I'm always the one they count on."

Impact of Control Talk

- Shows the situation is under control, when it works.

- Fosters resistance if it is experienced as "boxing in" the other. (Most people like to participate in conversations and decisions that affect them; few like to be ordered around.)

- Sometimes creates misunderstanding, distance, and tension in its commanding tone.

- Can generate a Fight-or Spite-Talk response, if it is perceived as abrasive or discounting.

- Excessive Control Talk may indicate mounting pressures.

> If Control Talk goes on constantly with one or both of you,
> power is a struggle in your relationship.

FIGHT TALK

Fight Talk strives to force change by intimidating others and defending self. It is an active, one-up, aggressive style — attempting power-over-other(s).

Intention to:
dominate
attack
criticize/blame
insult
bully
punish
avoid responsibility
hide fear/vulnerability
counter attack
bluff
win

Intention to be:
right
powerful
superior
justified
hurtful (sometimes)

II

Fight Talk

Mood
actively angry
anxious/tense
hostile/defiant
uncertain
disdainful

Nonverbals:
aggressive gestures
upper-body tension
"in your face" crowding
often loud, strident tone
abusive actions—
shouting , slapping,
hitting, throwing things,
slamming doors,
driving wrecklessly

Cue words:
"why" (to blame) questions
same as Control Talk with more
intensity and aggression
profanity and foul language

This talking style:

- Erupts around blocked desires or broken expectations.
- Covers emotions of disappointment, frustration, anxiety or fear.
- Focuses on persons rather than the issue.
- Discounts, devalues others, communicating a "damn-you" attitude.
- Ventilates, "acts out" anger.
- Is out of touch with self and other-awareness, consequently is out of control.

Typical Fight Talk Behaviors

Criticizing: "You never think before you act."

Defending: "I did it the right way, whether you think so or not."

Blaming, accusing, attacking, scolding: "It's your fault. You weren't paying attention."

Threatening, Intimidating: "I'll be watching every move you make."

Demanding, ordering: "Do it the way I say, or don't do it at all."

Arguing: "That's not right. It doesn't work that way."

Putting down, belittling, insulting, ridiculing: "If you had a brain in your head, you wouldn't know what to do with it."

Attributing, projecting: "All you think about is making money."

Pronouncing ultimatums: "Do that one more time and you've had it!"

Labeling, stereotyping: "You're lazy and irresponsible."

Name-calling: "Hey stupid, how many times do I have to tell you? That's not the way to do it!"

Bullying, challenging, taunting: "You can't take it! Come on, take a swing at me."

Impact of Fight Talk

- Gets juices flowing and may break up a logjam once in awhile.
- Breeds defensiveness, resistance, tension and stress in others.
- Fuels arguments that can escalate to physical violence, creating an unsafe environment.
- Leaves partner angry, wanting to get even.
- Ironically, gives away (loses) personal power.
- Often damages relationships by saying and doing mean and hurtful things that are later regretted.
- Blocks vital information and collaborative solutions to challenging issues.

> Fight Talk between you and your partner
> signals one or more unresolved issue(s).

SPITE TALK

Spite Talk is an indirect attempt to bring down someone or something. It is a passive, one-down, aggressive style — exerting power-under-other(s).

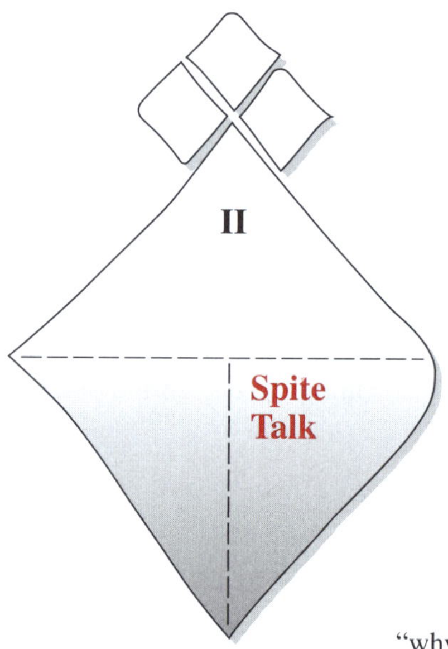

Intention to:
manipulate
protect self
humiliate
twist/distort
sound smart
get even/retaliate
undermine change
withhold information
hide agenda
ignore
show inequity

Intention to be:
deceitful
scornful
disrespectful
uncooperative
helpless/pitied
funny (with a bite)

Mood
angry undercurrent
resentful
contemptuous
disdainful
pessimistic
indifferent
disengaged/resigned
helpless/hopeless

Nonverbals:
sighs
rolling of the eyes
cynical/sarcastic tone
drooping posture
tense silence

Cue words:
they, it
"why" (to complain) questions
denials

People resort to spiteful messages when they believe they have no other way to influence others, or they have a hidden agenda.

This talking style:

- Is indirect and angry, often covering underlying hurt, distrust, or resentment.

- Exercises power as powerlessness — uses disengagement, passivity, non-compliance, sabotage, or retaliation to manipulate.

- Exerts control from "weakness," rather than from a position of strength.

- Discounts, devalues self, communicating a "poor-me" attitude.

- Often complicates issues by complaining inappropriately to a third person.

- Sees self as a "victim" rather than an "agent" who makes things happen.

- Can represent either a long-term personal lifestyle of low self-esteem, or a temporary, wounded response to a particular situation.

Typical Spite-Talk Behaviors

Shooting zingers, taking cheap shots: "If you're so smart, you do it."

Cynicism, sarcasm, disgust: "Look who claims to have all the answers."

Complaining, whining, implying "poor me, ain't it awful": "Nobody ever asks me what I think."

Nagging: "Do I always have to tell you to pick up your clothes?"

Pouting, withdrawing angrily, withholding affection: (going about business in silent unresponsiveness)

Making excuses: "Everybody else does it, too."

Stonewalling, refusing to answer when questioned

Denying, : "No, nothing's wrong. What makes you think that?"

Lying, distorting, misleading: "I called Pete yesterday (no call was made)."

Keeping score/reprisals: "I won't forget what you just said."

Giving in grudgingly, placating: "No, that's all right. Let's do it your way. I'm sure it will come out better than if we do what I want."

Being a martyr (covering for others, accepting blame): "It was probably my fault again. I should have . . . ."

Putting self down: "If I wasn't so dumb, I would have caught the mistake."

Attempt to humiliate, guilt, shame other: "I can't believe you did that."

Gossiping/being self-righteous: "I would never think of stooping that low."

Mean teasing: Mocking and poking fun at partner when the partner does not think it is funny.

Impact of Spite Talk

- Seeds and feeds conflict "under the table."
- Drains, diffuses energy and stifles creativity.
- Thwarts change and brings discouragement.

> Spite Talk between you and your partner
> signals one or more unresolved issue(s).

Connect, Collaborate, Develop

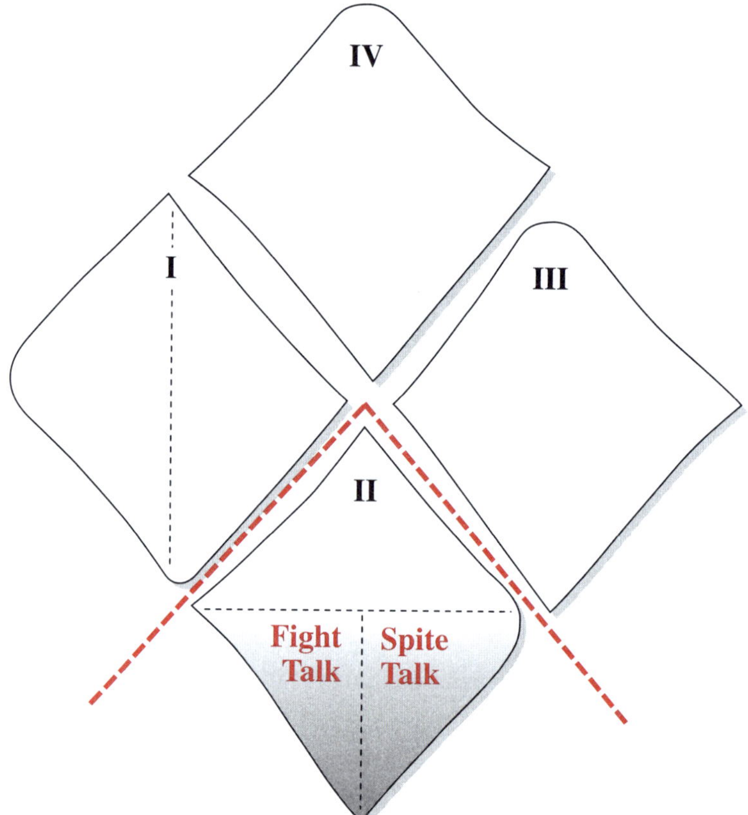

Command, Control, Defend

Both Fight Talk and Spite Talk:

- Broadcast anger.
- Impact health negatively.
- Maintain self-deception, if continued.
- Disregard self's contribution and response to the situation.
- Yield win/lose, or both-lose outcomes.

STYLE III — Search Talk

Search Talk is an open and rational way of talking. It examines facts, suggests

Intention to:
clarify
search for causes
provide perspective, insight
generate/brainstorm options
evaluate alternatives
propose solutions

III

Search Talk

Mood
calm
inquisitive
reflective

Nonverbals:
relaxed
laid back
gazing

Intention to be:
logical
expansive
flexible
insightful
safe
tentative

Cue words:
maybe, perhaps
could, might
possibly, probably
wonder, suppose
what if
why (without blame)

options, and gains an overview — to see the big picture.

This talking style:

- Provides a safe way to approach an issue that is non-routine, complex, or uncertain.

- Offers a good way to shift away from an argument (Style II), to reduce pressure, and to expand information.

- Focuses more on past or future time-frames than on the experience of the present.

- Lacks, by itself, commitment to future action.

Typical Search-Talk Behaviors

Identifying issues: "I'm wondering if we are letting work schedules crowd our time together."

Giving relevant background information: "Between us we carry about eight credit cards."

Analyzing, considering causes: "Maybe you're so fatigued at the end of a day because you aren't getting enough exercise."

Giving opinions, impressions, explanations: "I think we eat out too much."

Making interpretations, speculating: "Barb's phone call probably means she's feeling better."

Brainstorming, generating possibilities: "Perhaps you could set a time to jog every other day. How about playing tennis together twice a week?"

Making suggestions: "I suggest we think about it for a week or so."

Play out various scenarios without committing to any particular action: "If we got up fifteen minutes earlier in the morning, we could beat the traffic.

Posing solutions: "Suppose you go back to school in the fall. How do you think that would work?"

Impact of Search Talk

- Gets new ideas into the open.
- Becomes a "think-tank" to play out or expand options for the future.
- Risks skimming across the surface and missing important underlying emotional aspects of an issue.
- Can be a way to avoid resolving an issue in which neither partner takes responsibility for putting ideas into action.

> Your Search Talk as a couple shows your willingness to approach and deal with issues.

STYLE IV — Aware Talk

Aware Talk discloses all parts of a person's experience regarding a situation. This style reveals information left unsaid in other styles — typically feelings, wants, and commitments to act. It draws on power within and shares that power with other(s).

Intention to:
care about self and other
deal with "what is"
use self-awareness
engage other(s)
collaborate
take action

Intention to be:
clear
direct
honest/candid
responsible
accountable
respectful
tactful

IV

Aware Talk

Mood
involved
serious
safe

Nonverbals:
alert
present
focused
balanced
non-defensive

Cue words:
here and now orientation
speaking for self
emotions
want
will (commitment
to future action)

In Aware Talk, you go to the heart of an issue by:

- *Accessing* your own experience.
- *Accepting* what you find as *what is*, rather than disregard, deny, or run from it.
- *Owning* your own *contributions* and *responses* to an issue or situation.
- *Disclosing* your awareness honestly and skillfully.
- *Resolving* matters constructively.

In this talking style, you:

- Use your emotions constructively.
- Deal congruently with tension, differences, and conflict — without blaming, defending, or deceiving (Style II behaviors).
- Seek collaboration.
- Channel your energy into positive action.
- Manage self, rather than manipulate others.

Aware Talk:

- Is assertive and caring without being aggressive or defensive.

- Approaches with a softer tone, displaying a willingness to cooperate, rather than a harder, callused one.

- Enables you to discuss a difficult matter effectively if your intentions are to connect and collaborate rather than to command and control.

Typical Aware Talk Behaviors

Speaking for self — not for partner

Speaking about self, owning and sharing your own experience (using the Awareness Wheel and the six Talking Skills presented in chapter 3).

Identifying, anticipating issues: "Our recent spending scares me. I want to plan a way to rein it in."

Airing complaints: "When you say, 'Lets leave in 10 minutes,' and you are not ready for 30 minutes, that annoys me."

Taking responsibility for your own contribution/response: "Yeah, I didn't really listen to you. I assumed that I knew what you felt, so I started thinking about what to do next instead of listening."

Initiating, seeking change: "I'm frustrated with my job. I'd like to talk to you about making a career change."

Acknowledging differences: "My impression is that we are at opposite poles on this point."

Recognizing tension: "I'm feeling annoyed right now."

Revealing impact: "When you said that, I felt excited."

Giving support, disclosing wants for partner: "I've heard you say you want to go back to school and finish your degree. I'd like for you to have that happen."

Making an offer: "I'm willing to get the kids ready for bed tonight."

Committing to action, making and fulfilling promises: "Since that bothers you, I won't say it again."

Sharing hopes, dreams, plans: "I'd love to go back to school to prepare for a career change."

Giving encouraging feedback: "I thought you did a great job of standing up against my family's pressure. Good work!"

Requesting feedback: "Have you noticed, after I ask Matt for his ideas, whether I do something that prevents him from giving them?"

Disclosing vulnerability, weakness: "Basically, I don't feel as confident as I let on."

Giving feedback, requesting change: "I notice you often pull back and get quiet when I disagree with you. I'd rather you would tell me what's going on with you. What you are thinking and feeling?"

Repairing, apologizing, asking for forgiveness: "I really did hurt you by not including you. I'm sorry I did that. I want to apologize and assure you that I will not do that again."

Expressing appreciation: "Thank you for backing me up in our discussion with the kids. Your support made it easier for me not to be manipulated."

Impact of Aware Talk

- Results in deeper information and richer relationship.

- Builds trust as you share your real thoughts, feelings, and wants about issues.

- Demonstrates commitment to an open process, while bringing issues to closure.

- Can be transformational.

- Gets things done — is action oriented.

Aware Talk Brings Risk and Opportunity

- As you disclose more about yourself, you increase your listener's choices — what that person can do constructively or destructively about the information you supply.

- Usually disclosure begets disclosure and results in new understanding, intimacy and satisfaction.

> Using Aware Talk as a couple enables you to discuss things of importance to either or both of you at a deeper level.

YOUR BRAIN AND STYLES OF COMMUNICATION

The style of communication you use or choose at any point in time results from two forces: *instinct* and *learning,* both of which reside in your mind-brain. Three distinct but interconnected levels, with interrelated modules, form the whole of your brain. Each of these areas — action, emotional, and thinking subsystems — represent a particular function.

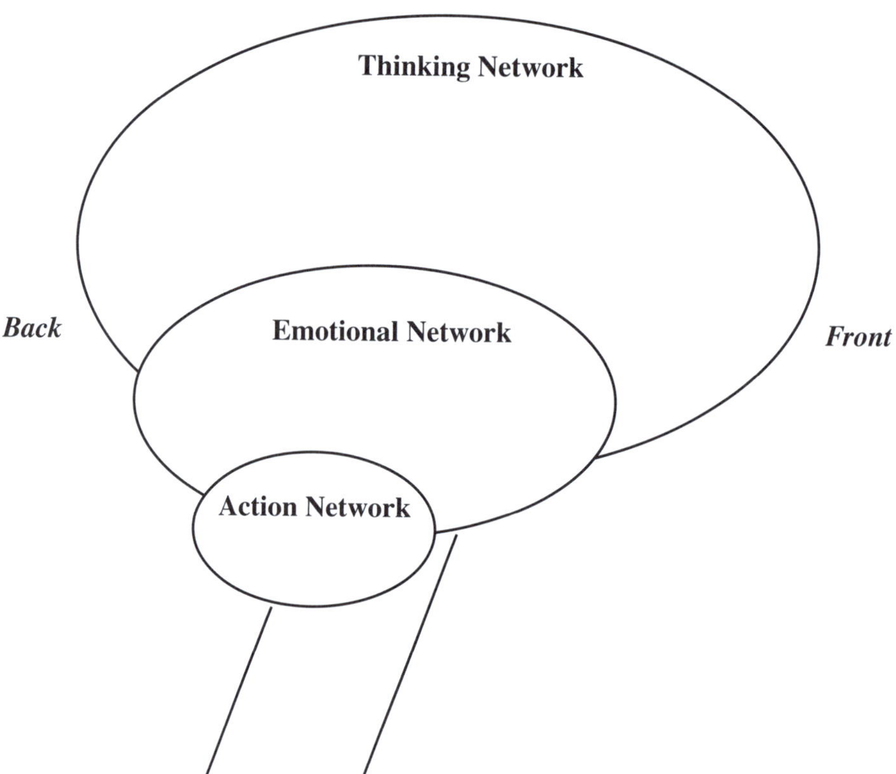

Your Action Network

The brainstem rests at the top of the spinal cord, at the base of the brain. The configuration is referred to as the "root brain." This area transfers action to the body. This network:

- Cannot think or feel.

- Is preset to regulate many basic bodily functions, such as respiration and metabolism, to ensure survival.

- Implements behavior.

Your Emotional Network

The second level, middle area of the brain, houses emotional circuitry. It is comprised of what is often called the limbic system. This emotional center:

- Generates our range of emotions and impulses, from feelings of fear, anxiety, and anger to sexual excitement, surprise and sadness. It dials down with feelings of happiness and joy.

- Reads another person's emotions through nonverbals.

- Gives us capacity to connect or empathize with someone else's emotion.

- Holds our ability to remember and learn.

- Is always "on" — alert and constantly monitoring our physical and social environments.

- Is primarily *reflexive*, ready to react to any sign of threat or danger.

Your Thinking Network

The third and highest level of the brain contains the thinking subsystem — the large area at the top of your brain — called the neocortex. This network:

- Enables you to expand awareness, think abstractly and comprehend.

- Gives the ability to access and analyze information, plan, and execute actions.

- Can consider, regulate, and talk about the emotional networks's experience.

- Is involved in the transmission of cultural knowledge and moral development.

- Has the potential to operate collaboratively with conscious intent, a high order of social activity and relationship.

- Is *reflective* in nature, allowing you to respond, rather than simply react.

THE "LOW ROAD" AND THE "HIGH ROAD"

Neuroscientists speak of two general pathways for processing information in the brain. These can be referred to as two roads.

One pathway goes immediately through the circuitry of the emotional brain, down to the root brain, to action. This route, called the *low road,* is:

- Reflexive and reactive.

- Largely unconscious and instinctual.

- Your "default system," ready for a fight or flight reaction.

- Very powerful and able to overwhelm and limit the executive functions of the thinking brain.

- Expressed in Fight Talk and Spite Talk — communicating the distressed, aggressive and defensive aspects of the emotional brain.

The other pathway activates the networks of the thinking brain to process information and provide choices of behavior. This avenue, called the *high road,* is:

- Reflective and proactive.

- Consciously aware, creative and potentially collaborative.

- Capable of integrating and managing powerful drives and emotions originating in the middle brain subsystem.

- Active in Search and Aware Talk.

Note

- The low road is fast, communicating nonverbally. The high road is slower, generating words.

- More neural pathways run from the emotional brain to the thinking brain, than run from the thinking brain to the emotional brain. This is partly why emotions can be overwhelming and sometimes difficult to manage.

- The low road comes naturally. The high road does not. It requires learning.

> Taking the "high road" enables you to deal
> with life's challenges effectively.

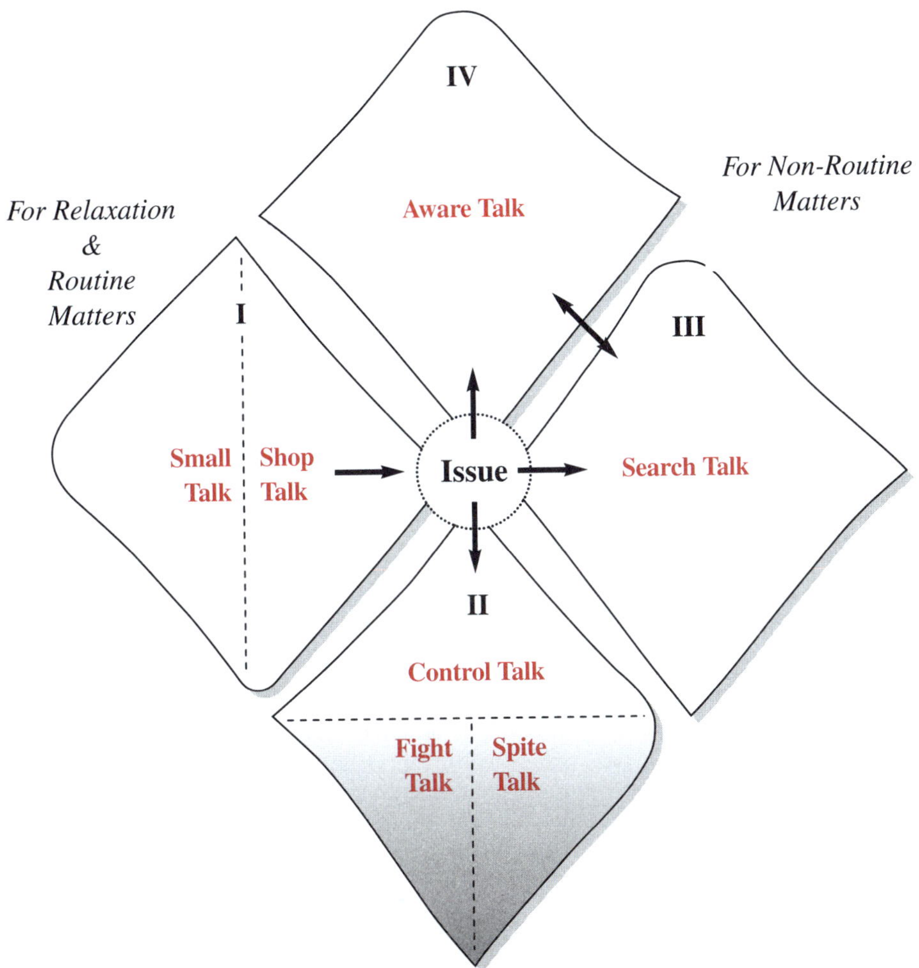

STYLES AND ROADS

Your style of communication in dealing with an issue reflects your mind-brain functioning — taking the "low road" or the "high road."

HANDLING LIFE'S CHALLENGES WITH THE ROAD YOU TAKE

Style I

Hopefully you spend a good portion of your time in a calm, confident, and happy state reflected in your use of Small Talk. You can make your time productive with Shop Talk. Style I is generally used to relax, reconnect, or handle daily routines.

Style II — Takes the Low Road

However, from time to time an "alarm goes off" in your mind and body. The alarm system housed in the emotional network of your brain, signals caution, novelty, change, potential threat or even danger. This more or less anxious and uncertain state typically means a potential issue is at hand. (This is shown in the graphic on page 31 with an arrow pointing from Style I to "Issue" in the center of the graphic.)

The alarm can be set off by a comment from your partner or some other external source, as well as by a memory or an imagined event. Your first and natural emotional brain reflex is to become defensive and reactive, to protect yourself in the face of uncertainty. (This is shown in the graphic by the arrow pointing from "Issue" to Style II.)

Control Talk — taking charge and giving directives — is the easiest and most efficient way to attempt to deal with the alarm. When it works (and others comply with your directives) the emotional center of your brain relaxes. You return to a calm and confident state. Often however, in interactive situations, your Control Talk is by-passed or does not work, and you jump into Fight Talk to attack directly, or you slide indirectly into Spite Talk to "hit and run."

When you go into Fight or Spite Talk, the emotional part of your brain has taken charge. It becomes more difficult to think clearly. Intentions of caring are pushed aside for control and self-protection.

If you allow your emotional brain to overwhelm you, often it takes a "time out" to calm and rebalance yourself. This gives the opportunity for you to reflect on the situation, and then you can shift to a more productive style of communication.

In interpersonal situations at home or at work, Fight and Spite Talk reactions usually do not solve things. Instead, they typically make matters worse, escalate a conflict, and often result in relational damage and personal regret.

Style III — Starts the High Road

When a non-routine matter arises, rather than being driven by the raw emotion, it is possible to shift to thinking and talking about the issue using Search Talk. As you do so, you use your mind to reflect on the situation, speculate about what is going on, and possibly generate a solution. (This is shown in the graphic on page 31 with the arrow pointing from "Issue" to Style III.)

Search Talk is a safe way to initiate a conversation and to buy time to think about things, without necessarily taking action. In the process, you redirect your emotions from defensive action to cooperative acton.

Style IV — Travels the High Road

To fully understand and resolve an issue, your thinking brain must incorporate and integrate important information from your emotional brain. The interactive process between the thinking part and the emotional part of your brain expands self-awareness and partner-awareness. This action also builds relationship confidence, trust, and intimacy. (This is shown in the graphic by the arrowing pointing from "Issue" to Style IV.)

Aware Talk employs all of your conscious faculties to deal effectively with an issue/situation. It generates the richest information without attacking or defending anyone. Out of this, you can develop congruent, satisfactory, and action-oriented resolutions. You use your awareness to act constructively, to learn, and to grow. This road becomes the path to a strong and secure couple bond.

Styles III and IV Together

Using a combination of Styles III and IV during a discussion about a *non-routine* matter is foundational to collaborative conversation and process. (This is shown on the graphic by an arrow with two points going between Styles III and IV.)

CHOOSE HOW YOU COMMUNICATE

Understanding communication styles shows what the possibilities are for dealing with issues — effectively and ineffectively. This is particularly important to know when you are under pressure or when a conflict arises. You can learn how to communicate and relate in constructive ways, taking the "high road" to meet the challenges of life.

After a chapter explaining issues, the rest of the workbook provides practical maps, skills, and processes — tools for activating the thinking part of your brain — using the high road. These tools increase your choices for relating collaboratively. They serve to expand self-awareness and partner-awareness so you and your partner can create a satisfying and fulfilling life together.

MY TALKING STYLES

Instructions

Step 1. Think of the talking styles you use when you are conversing with your partner. Estimate the percentage of time you *typically* spend in each of the styles. Then, if you would like to change how you talk with your partner, put a plus (+) in the style(s) you want to increase and a minus (—) in the ones you want to decrease.

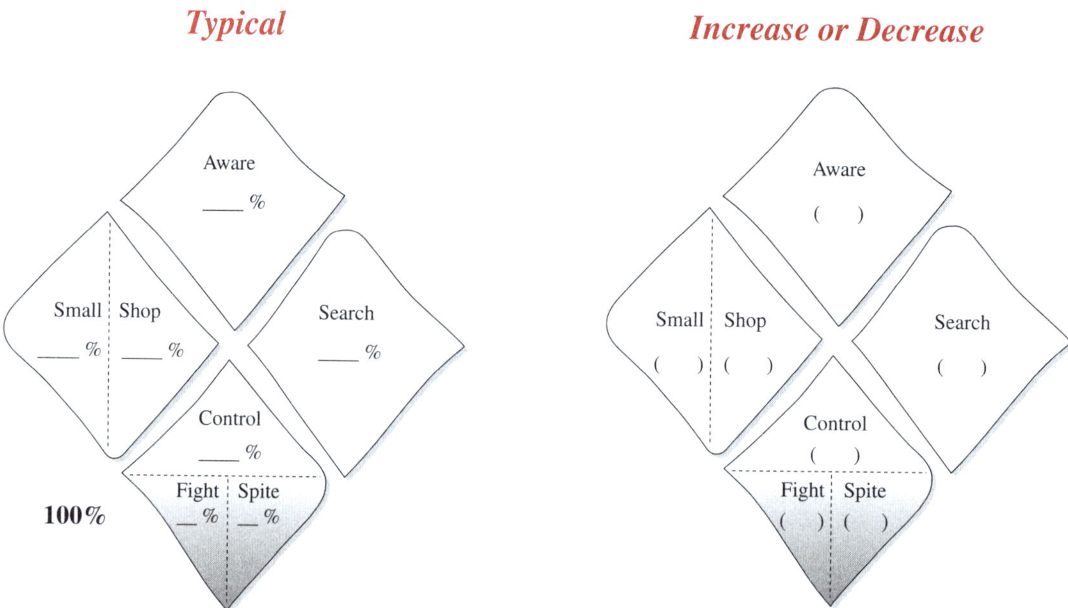

Step 2. Complete the worksheet on the next page, "My Partner's Talking Styles."

MY PARTNER'S TALKING STYLES

Instructions

Step 2 continued. Think of the talking styles your partner uses when he or she is conversing with you. Estimate the percentage of time he or she *typically* spends in each of the styles. If you would like your partner to alter his or her talking style, put a plus (+) in the style(s) you want increased and a minus (—) in the ones you want decreased.

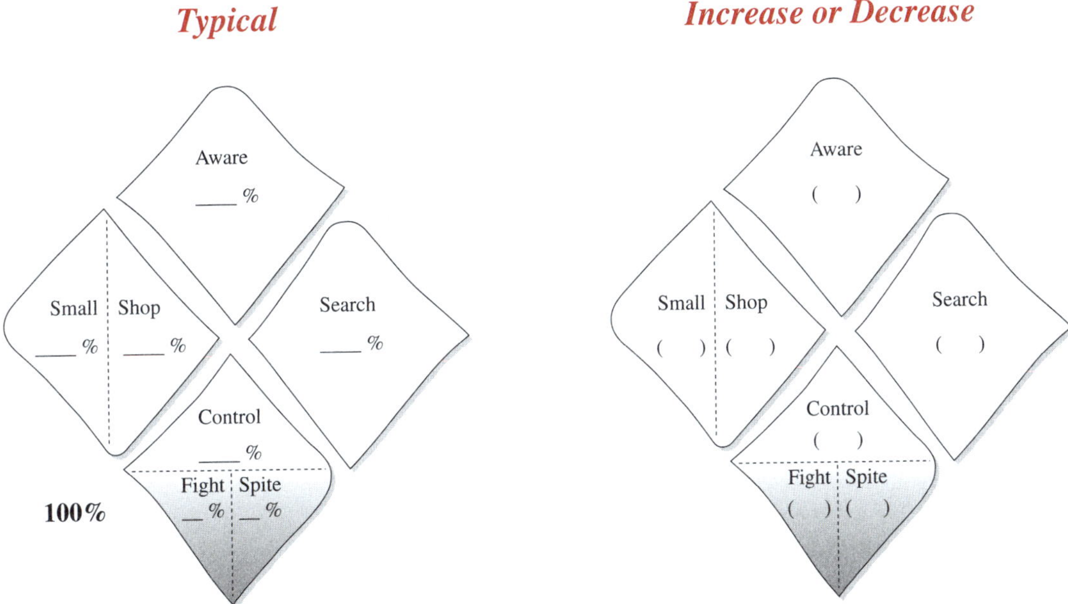

Step 3. After you and your partner both have completed these two pages, sit together, compare and discuss your perspectives.

Step 4. Jointly decide when and where you can implement the changes you desire.

BETWEEN-SESSION APPLICATIONS

Do the following activities prior to the next COUPLE COMMUNICATION session.

THRIVE Sphere

If you and your partner have not yet taken THRIVE, the on-line Collaborative Marriage Sphere, you are encouraged to do so before the next session. See pages v-vi in the Introduction to this workbook for details.

Observe Others:

In the coming week, pay attention to the communication styles you encounter at home or with other people — at work, on television, with friends, or in public. As you observe and mentally identify the styles, notice what impact they have on the people involved and on anyone close by.

Monitor Self:

In the days ahead, pay attention to your own use of talking styles — at home and with others, such as with people at work. Notice the effect of the styles you use on the people with whom you interact.

Apply Scripture:

Return to the scripture verses given at the front of this chapter. Review and reflect on them, in relation to your own styles of talking. Determine if there is one verse that is particularly helpful for you to keep in mind. If there is, note it or commit it to memory, to draw upon when a situation arises to which it applies.

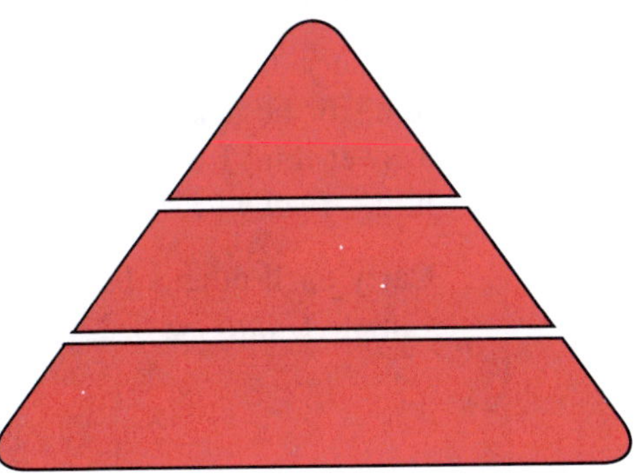

CHAPTER 2

Scripture for Considering Issues

When concerns arise in your life, consider these words of scripture:

"For I know the plans I have for you," declares the Lord, "plans to prosper you and not to harm you, plans to give you hope and a future." *Jeremiah 29:11*

Come to me, all you who are weary and burdened, and I will give you rest. Take my yoke upon you and learn from me, for I am gentle and humble in heart, and you will find rest for your souls. For my yoke is easy and my burden is light. *Matthew 11: 28-30*

Do not be anxious about anything, but in everything, by prayer and petition, with thanksgiving, present your requests to God. And the peace of God, which transcends all understanding, will guard your hearts and your minds in Christ Jesus. *Philippians 4:6-7*

"Because he loves me," says the Lord, "I will rescue him; I will protect him, for he acknowledges my name. He will call upon me, and I will answer him; I will be with him in trouble, I will deliver him and honor him." *Psalm 91:14-15*

Carry each other's burdens, and in this way you will fulfill the law of Christ. *Galatians 6:2*

2

Types of Issues
The Third Force

In the course of life, issues arise for everyone. These attention-getters emerge out of normal, daily situations and vary according to your stage in life. They crop up, for example, when you have a baby, change jobs, or move from one place to another — at times when circumstances change or opportunities appear. Issues erupt when something unexpected happens, including a crisis. They surface as you and your partner anticipate the future and make plans together.

If an issue is present, your experiences relating to it and the details of it often become the content of your conversation. It also can generate a conflict. As a couple, when you handle your common concerns — whether small or large issues— effectively, you can prevent conflicts from developing between you, or you can resolve the conflicts that do occur more satisfactorily. Skills give you the means to accomplish these ends.

As you learn the communication skills in this program, you are encouraged to practice the skills on and apply them to your own issues. To give perspective (and provide guidance in selecting issues for practice), the following definition, framework, and examples may be helpful.

ISSUES — Life's Concerns and Opportunities

An issue is anything (behavior, event, information, situation, opportunity, or challenge) that concerns or is important to you or your partner. It usually involves making a decision.

Types

The issues you face, at one time or another, fall into three categories:

- Topical — about places, things, events, or tasks

- Personal — about yourself (or about your partner) as an individual

- Relational — between people (between yourself *and* your partner, or between yourself *and* another person, such as another family member)

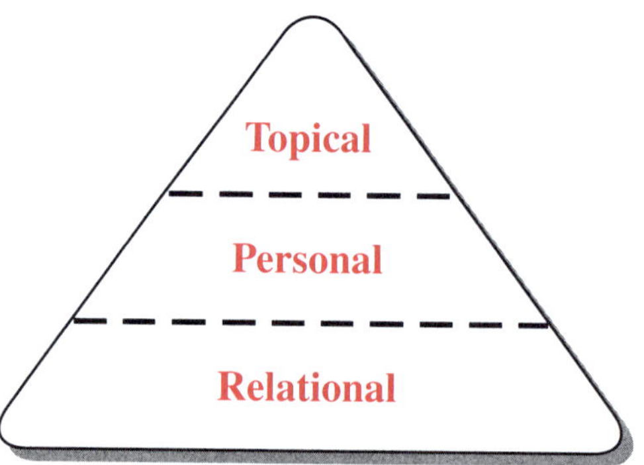

Consider These Points

- You may think of an issue as fitting into a single category, which usually is the case. However, an issue is not always this neatly packaged. Sometimes it is composed of a combination of types. In these instances, the categories interrelate and impact each other. For example, say you have an issue about earning extra money (topical) to go back to school in order to advance your career (personal); these plans could bring up the issue of time you spend together with your partner (relational).

- Issues tend to increase in importance and consequence as the focus moves from topical to relational.

- Issues require varying amounts of mental, emotional, and physical energy to resolve, depending on their significance.

TYPES OF ISSUES — Examples

Topical

Children	Food	In-Laws/	Parenting	Roles	Time
Clothes	Friends	Relatives	Parents	Shopping	Transportation
Credit Cards	Gambling	Internet	Pets	Sports	Travel
Drugs/	Holidays	Leisure/	Politics	Stepfamily	Vacation
Alcohol	Housework	Recreation	Pornography	Television	Yardwork
Ex-spouse	Housing	Money	Projects	Tobacco	

Personal

Appearance	Exercise	Goals	Job/Work	Responsibility	Stress
Attitude	Energy	Grief	Personal	Risky	Success
Career	Failure	Health	Habits	Behaviors	Values
Confidence	Faith/	Identity	Productivity	Self-	Volunteerism
Education	Religion	Integrity	Recognition	Discipline	Weight

Relational

Acceptance	Competition	Forgiveness	Power/	Satisfaction	Violence/
Affection	Conflict	Fun	Control	Separation	Abuse
Boundaries	Decision-	Infidelity	Respect	Support	
Celebration	making	Intimacy	Sexuality	Time	
Commitment	Differences	Influence	Sacrifice	Together	
Communication	Equality	Loyalty	Safety	Trust	

- Knowing the differences among types of issues can help you identify and deal with your issues more clearly and effectively.

INVENTORY OF CURRENT ISSUES

Date: _______________________

Instructions

Take a few minutes, relax, and think about what is going on in your life at the present time. Think about your activities at home, work, and elsewhere. As you reflect, write down a word or phrase that represents the *topical, personal,* or *relational* concerns that come to your mind. (If something is too private for this setting, you may choose not to write it down.)

If you have taken THRIVE: The Collaborative Marriage Profile, list any issues or conflicts identified in the THRIVE Report that you believe would be useful to tackle.

Issues

THE THIRD FORCE

In any conversation about issues, three forces are at work:

- The content — what it is all about — your experience and the information related to it.

- The outcome — a solution that fits.

- The process — how you talk and listen to one another (your communication style).

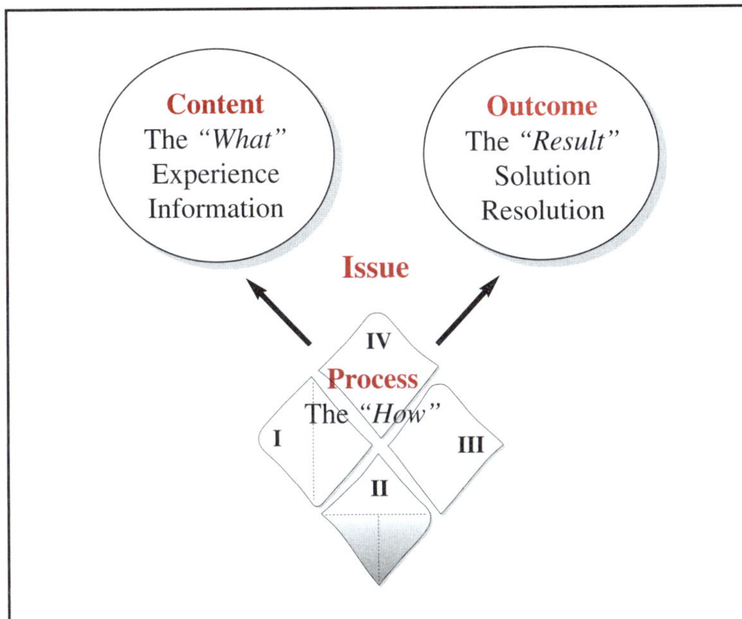

Most couples simply focus on the content or the outcome, without attention to the process. While all three forces are important, the biggest influence on the quality of the content expressed and the outcome developed is the process used. *Collaborative Marriage Skills* develops process skills for enhancing both the content and the outcome of your conversations. These skills take you to the high road as you handle the issues of life.

> To improve the quality of content and outcome,
> improve the process.

CHAPTER 3

Scripture for Using Your Awareness Wheel

Scripture speaks of what is inside of you — the awareness you can gain of yourself. Plus, it gives guidance on the way you talk. Consider what it says in the verses below:

The Lord does not look at the things man looks at. Man looks at the outward appearance, but the Lord looks at the heart. *I Samuel 16:7b*

The Lord searches every heart and understands every motive behind the thoughts. *I Chronicles 28:9b*

Surely you desire truth in the inner parts; you teach me wisdom in the inmost place. Create in me a pure heart, O God, and renew a steadfast spirit within me. *Psalm 51:6 and 51:10*

Truthful lips endure forever, but a lying tongue lasts only a moment. *Proverbs 12:19*

Be transformed by the renewing of your mind. Then you will be able to test and approve what God's will is — his good, pleasing and perfect will. *Romans 12: 2b*

Test me, O Lord, and try me, examine my heart and my mind. *Psalm 26:2*

Speaking the truth in love, we will in all things grow up into him who is the Head, that is, Christ. *Ephesians 4:15*

If I speak in the tongues of men and of angels, but have not love, I am only a resounding gong or a clanging cymbal. *I Corinthians 13:1*

A man finds joy in giving an apt reply — and how good is a timely word! *Proverbs 15:23*

The Lord detests lying lips, but he delights in men who are truthful. *Proverbs 12:22*

Therefore each of you must put off falsehood and speak truthfully . . . for we are all members of one body. *Ephesians 4:25*

May the words of my mouth and the meditation of my heart be pleasing in your sight, O Lord, my Rock and my Redeemer. *Psalm 19:14*

3

Awareness Wheel Map
Self-Talk
6 Talking Skills

Awareness — understanding yourself and your partner accurately, especially in relation to issues and situations — is foundational to effective communication. This chapter gives you a tool to unlock and increase your self awareness.

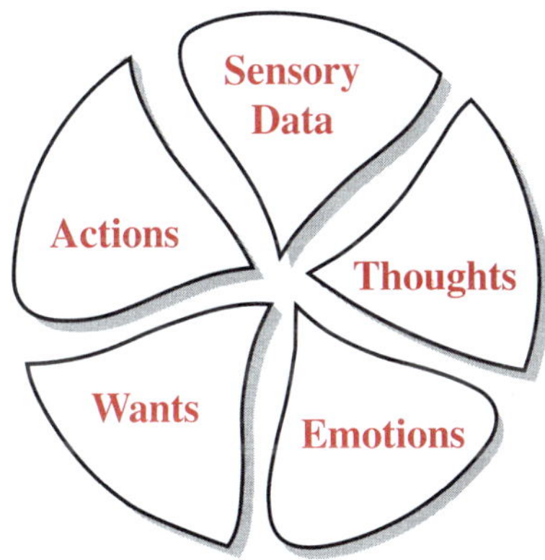

The tool, called the Awareness Wheel, is actually a map of your experience of an issue or situation. The map helps you to reflect on and clarify, at any moment in time, how you are responding to the issue. The tool is particularly useful when a conflict arises. It gives you the means to travel the high road — to relate in ways that care for yourself and your partner.

HOW YOU EXPERIENCE AN ISSUE

All issues — whether topical, personal, or relational — have an underlying, common structure. They are made up of five different types of information. Similar to the way a simple sentence contains basic parts — subject, verb, and object — your experience of an issue contains basic parts — your sensory data, thoughts, emotions, wants, and actions. The Awareness Wheel map presents the parts in an overall structure.

Each of the five parts — or zones —of the Awareness Wheel contains important information about yourself. The parts are:

- Distinct qualitatively.

- Connected, impacting one another.

- Present, whether or not you are conscious of them.

- Useful particularly when you tune into them.

Through its function as a map, the Awareness Wheel represents and integrates your whole brain — your root, emotional, and thinking brain areas. The following sections describe each of the zones of the Wheel and then explain how to use the map as a practical tool.

> The most important resource you bring to any situation is your ability to tune in to your own awareness.

PARTS OF THE AWARENESS WHEEL

SENSORY DATA — Inputs to You

Sensory Data are pieces of information you receive via your five senses: sight, sound, smell, taste, and touch. They are what you perceive.

External Sources

You receive, through the five channels, non-verbal and verbal data about your partner and other people. What you take in includes their:

actions	gestures	scent	pitch/pace/tone
facial expressions	posture	silence	words

Your brain also scans your environment constantly to pick up data from other sources, such as:

- Context — time, place — the surroundings.
- Electronic media and printed materials.

Internal Sources

Sensory data come to your awareness from inside your own body, as well. These include:

- Physical sensations — for example, the lack or presence of physical pain, muscle relaxation or tension, fatigue, hunger or fullness (satiation).
- Specific memories.
- Visualization, imagination — imagery of the future.
- Remembered dreams.

Functions of External and Internal Sources

Your five senses give you the ability to have:

- Immediate and historical (recalled) contact with your world.
- Details for describing (documenting) your observations.
- Imagined pictures (visualizations) of future possibilities.

The more observant you become to the details of your sensory data, the better you will become at using your own "database" effectively.

THOUGHTS — The Meaning You Make

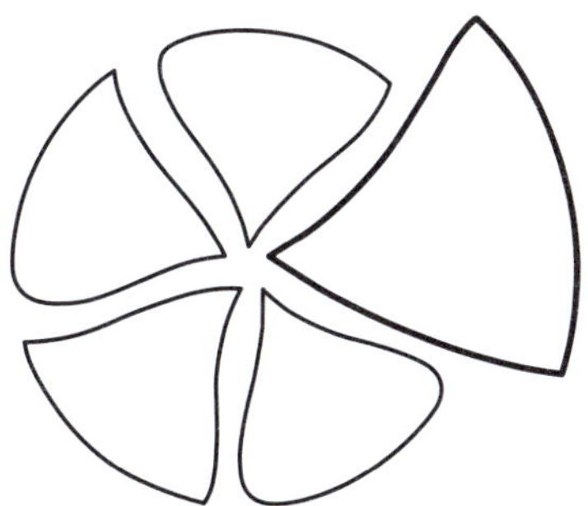

Thoughts are the meanings you make out of the sensory data you receive.

The following four forms of thoughts correspond generally with your past, present, and future thinking:

- *Beliefs/assumptions* — what you hold to be true, useful, and valuable from your past experience that you bring to each new situation.

- *Interpretations* — the meaning or appraisal you make currently of sensory data. This includes logical and analytical processes of weighing data, as well as irrational (biased and distorted) thinking. Interpretations represent the way you put your world together at any point in time.

- *Expectations* — the future you anticipate or what you think will happen, based on what you have seen or heard — perceived — from some current or past sensory data. Expectations function as "future memories" — waiting to be fulfilled.

- *Possibilities* — the future you imagine — alternative ways of viewing the future.

Other words that signal thinking processes include:

ascriptions	constraints	impressions	potentials
assessments	convictions	judgments	predictions
benefits	evaluations	metaphors	prejudices
biases	guesses	needs	principles
conclusions	hunches	opinions	reasons
consequences	ideas	objections	values

Points to Consider:

- Beliefs, interpretations, expectations, and possibilities are powerful forces. They are strong influences on your decisions and actions, and they can limit or expand what you do.

- Sometimes thoughts can be quite illogical or inconsistent with the evidence.

- It is possible to create (add), select (filter), or ignore (delete) pieces of sensory data to fit your beliefs, interpretations, and expectations. This results in bias and distortion.

- Thoughts often become self-fulfilling prophesies.

- Your self-esteem arises from your beliefs and judgments about yourself in various circumstances across time.

- Your partner may see and hear the same data and come to very different conclusions.

- In addition to sensory data, other parts of the Awareness Wheel affect your thoughts.

Emotions — Your Feelings

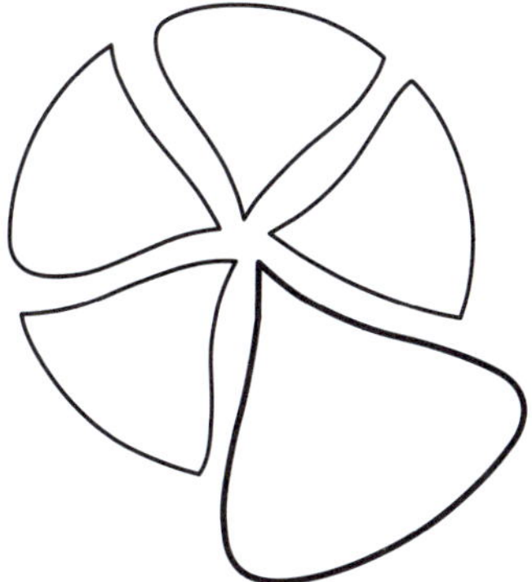

Emotions are the body's response to the interpretation of sensory data. Emotions are *alerted* by external or internal sensory inputs, which are quickly *appraised* to be safe or dangerous, pleasant or unpleasant. They *arouse* readiness to act — typically approach or withdrawal behavior.

Many of your emotions operate below the conscious level. They impact your chemistry, blood pressure, heart rate, and muscle tension and are observable externally as non-verbal behaviors — facial expressions, bodily movements, or voice tone and intensity.

Upon reflection, emotions can be raised to consciousness where they can be considered, named, and managed. In many situations, you experience several different kinds of emotions at the same time.

Six Basic Emotions

Each of these six basic emotions is recognized non-verbally across cultures:

happiness   sadness   anger   fear   disgust   surprise

Other variations of emotions occur, as well. For example, you can feel:

amazed	delighted	frightened	peaceful
annoyed	disappointed	frustrated	pleased
anxious	discouraged	glad	proud
ashamed	eager	guilty	relieved
calm	elated	hurt	resentful
cautious	embarrassed	irritated	satisfied
comfortable	enthusiastic	jealous	scared
contented	excited	joyful	uneasy

Understanding Emotions

Emotions reflect what is happening in other parts of your Awareness Wheel. (Feelings do not just come out of the blue.) For this reason, emotions are quite rational and predictable. This is why you can learn to trust your emotions as useable information.

For example, if what you hear (sensory data) matches or mismatches your expectations (thoughts), your corresponding emotions — from pleasing to disturbing — occur. If you hear that a particular job offer goes to someone else and you were expecting to receive that offer, you might feel disappointed, angry, and jealous. On the other hand, you might feel a little relieved, if part of you believes the job might be over your head or too demanding. The stronger your expectations, the stronger the resulting feelings.

Emotions have multi-functions:

- Like an alarm, they signal new or unresolved issues — that something is unsettling — originating in some zone of your Wheel.

- They are the internal indicators (feedback) of your level of satisfaction with the *process* (handling) and the *outcome* (result) of an issue.

Your body gives you clues to your emotions. If you tune into your body's internal sensations, you can often locate where you feel your emotions. For example, you may recognize a certain sensation in your stomach when you are excited or afraid. Your upper body muscles tighten with distress or anger. Your muscles relax with the feelings of happiness and peace.

Making Use of Emotions:

- Emotions regulate and direct the flow of energy through your body.

- Since emotions are part of *what is*, they do not have to be justified, denied, or avoided. If you do not attend to them, you miss important information that is essential for making good decisions or resolving conflicts.

- If your emotions are not distorted by drugs (sometimes including prescription drugs), alcohol, organic disease, or confused learning, your feelings function like an accurate gauge — a barometer. They give you a reliable reading of your situation.

- Emotions lend color to dry logic and cold facts.

- Even though your emotions occur outside your conscious control, once you gain awareness of them, you increase your ability to manage them. As you recognize and acknowledge them, you can learn ways to control yourself and express them appropriately.

Many people use the phrase, "I feel like" or "I feel that" and believe they are giving an emotion, however, they are really giving a thought. While using the word *feel* for *think* is common in our language, this use does not distinguish adequately your emotions from your thoughts. The two kinds of information are qualitatively distinct. Confusing the two limits the clarity of your awareness and the effectiveness of your communication.

Three examples of the confusion include:
> "I feel like I'm *competent*."
> "I feel that I'm *rejected*."
> "I feel *threatened*."

These are really thoughts, which in these cases are evaluations of yourself or a situation. Notice what happens when you consider *competent*, *rejected* or *threatened* as thoughts, and not emotions: You become actively in charge of your thinking (your evaluations), and aware of your associated emotions. For example:

> "I believe I'm competent. I feel confident and pleased.

> "I think I'm being rejected. I feel disappointed and discouraged."

> "I have a hunch I'm being threatened. I'm scared and angry."

When an issue is involved, most thoughts have one or more feelings associated with them, or vice versa. Thoughts that typically produce considerable emotion are easy to confuse with feelings. For richer awareness and clearer communication, pay attention to the difference between your thoughts and your feelings.

Below is a partial list of some *thought words that are commonly expressed as emotions.* As you read over the list, identify the emotions (sometimes strong emotions) that often accompany these thoughts:

Betrayed	Dominated	Rejected
Challenged	Important	Respected
Cheated	Inadequate	Rewarded
Childish	Intimidated	Slighted
Competent	Incompetent	Tempted
Conspicuous	Insulted	Threatened
Deceitful	Persecuted	Thwarted
Defeated	Pressured	Unappreciated

WANTS — Your Desires

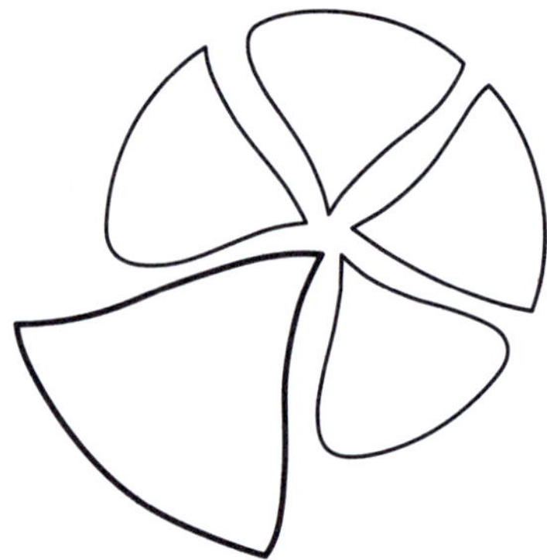

Wants are your wishes and intentions for yourself and for others, short-term or long-term, and general or specific.

Other common words associated with wants include:

aspirations	goals	longings
dreams	hopes	motives
drives	incentives	objectives

Three types of wants, with examples, include:

- *To be*: healthy, honest, respected, appreciated, liked, successful.
- *To do* — general or specific

    General: compete, collaborate, get even, clarify, support

    Specific: finish a project, change jobs, go out to dinner
- *To have*: more time, a different car, good friends

Wants:

- Sometimes start vaguely and then become more specific.
- Vary in intensity from weak to strong.
- Reflect your values.
- Provide direction without commitment to action. They imply a movement towards or away from something or someone.
- Remain tentative, as intentions to act, until they are translated into future actions —next steps. By themselves, wants do not necessarily change things.

What You Want Comes Out Directly or Indirectly in Your Actions.

- You can have multiple wants, and they can either converge or compete with one another.

- When your wants are fragmented or conflicting, they scatter your energy and lead to incongruent behavior.

- Hidden wants (perhaps because they are not acceptable to yourself or others important to you) become hidden agenda. They result in confusing, misleading, or dishonest communication.

- Clarifying and prioritizing your wants can help focus your energy.

Wants *for* Versus *from*

When we attend to wants, we often first think of self: my interests, what I desire *for* myself. This demonstrates caring about self (which is important to recognize). When it comes to thinking about others, it is easy to think only about what I want *from* others (*for* self) — not *for* others (and particularly my partner), based on his or her interests.

Wants for:

S	O	U
Self	**Other(s)**	**Us**
Myself	My Partner Other Persons Involved	Our Relationship

Wants *for* Other(s) Builds Bridges

Wants *for* other(s) means wanting for the others, to the extent possible, what you have heard them say they want (your sensory data).

The Big Test

The big test is: Do your wants *for the other* match what the other wants for himself or herself? A match passes the test.

- If you do not know what your partner wants, ask him or her.

- If you cannot support all your partner's wants, at least acknowledge them and look for wants you can support. Usually, something exists around which you can connect and build.

- Caution: It is easy to want *for* others what you think would be good for them (what they *should* want). This does not pass the test. (It often reflects a want for self.)

- Wants for the other requires real understanding of another, truly hearing his or her stated interests.

Wants for Relationship

Wants for your relationship are *wants that both of you can buy into* for the good of your relationship.

Needs Versus Wants

Sometimes people use the word *need* to express a *want*. For example, "I need to have you . . ."; however, a need usually states an evaluation (a thought) about an impending situation. Often a stated need implies a demand rather than a desire or want, which is more negotiable. For this reason, needs are placed in the thought zone of the Awareness Wheel. Be careful not to confuse needs with wants.

Motivation — Putting Wants to Work for You

- Everyone has wants and wants are motivators. If you want to motivate someone, discover his or her interests, and integrate those with yours.

- When you help your partner achieve his or her objectives, you strengthen your relationship.

Caring for Self, Partner, and Relationship Expressed in Wants

- While sometimes challenging, affirming wants for your partner demonstrates love and caring.

- When each partner's wants are being seriously considered — and to the extent possible, incorporated — you can resolve issues faster.

- Wants for partner are at the heart of a collaborative marriage.

ACTIONS — Your Behavior

Actions are what you do and say — your nonverbal behavior and verbal statements

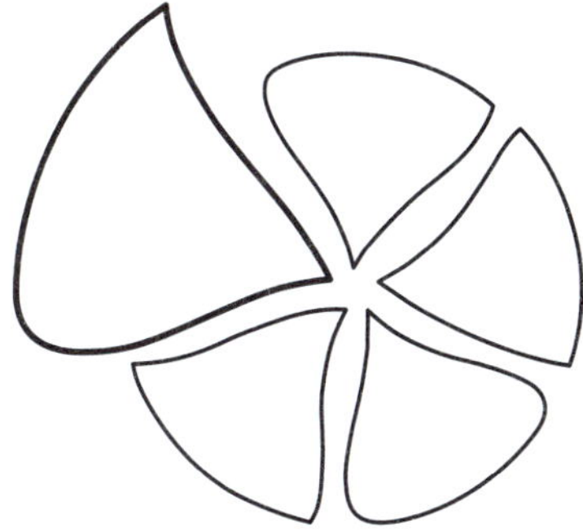

— past, present, and future.

External Actions

Most actions are overt and observable, the resulting *output* of how you *process* your experience — sensory data, thoughts, emotions, and wants — consciously or unconsciously.

Internal Actions

Other actions occur internally and are typically less observable. For example, considering, reflecting, believing, trusting, worrying, listening, doubting, agreeing or disagreeing are all internal actions.

Importance of Stating Your Actions

- Past Action: What you did or said earlier — yesterday, last week, last year, or before — *yields accountability.*

- Current Action: What you do or say currently — *exhibits responsibility.*

- Expressing Future Action: what you will do at a specific point in time — an hour from now, tomorrow, or next week — puts will into motion and *proclaims commitment.*

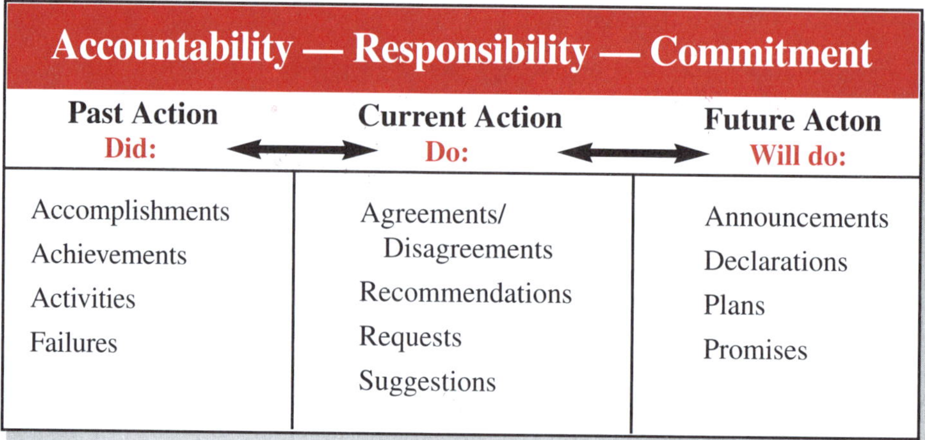

Points to Consider

- Your actions (output) become sensory data (input) for others, such as your partner.

- Trust is built or destroyed through keeping or breaking commitments.

- People are known by the promises they keep. Take your future-action statements seriously.

EARLY WARNING SIGNALS TO ISSUES

A signal to an issue can come from any zone of your Awareness Wheel:

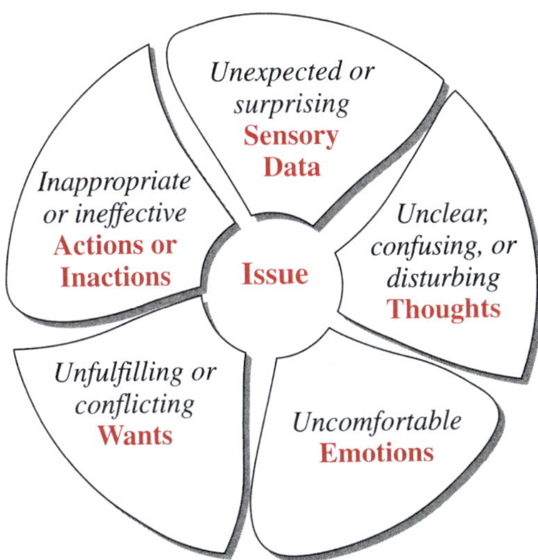

The Awareness Wheel can be used to alert you to an issue, to reflect on it, and to resolve it. One way to do any of these activities occurs through your Self-Talk, as described in the following section.

SELF-TALK: PROCESSING AN ISSUE INTERNALLY

Self-talk is your internal conversation — the process of connecting with all parts of yourself in order to resolve an issue.

Using the Awareness Wheel for Self-Talk

The Awareness Wheel works as a tool to "self-talk" your way through an issue. To use it:

- Privately ask yourself, "What is going on right now? What am I experiencing?"

- Develop and organize your awareness to analyze the issue.

- Cover all parts of the Wheel in any order — fill in any blind spots (missing information).

- Be honest with yourself. Accept what you find as where you are — the starting point for dealing with the issue.

- Keep expanding your awareness and reflecting on the issue until you make sense of all the parts and are able to choose a constructive next step (future action). A future action can be a small next step. (Do not keep doing what you have been doing that has not worked.)

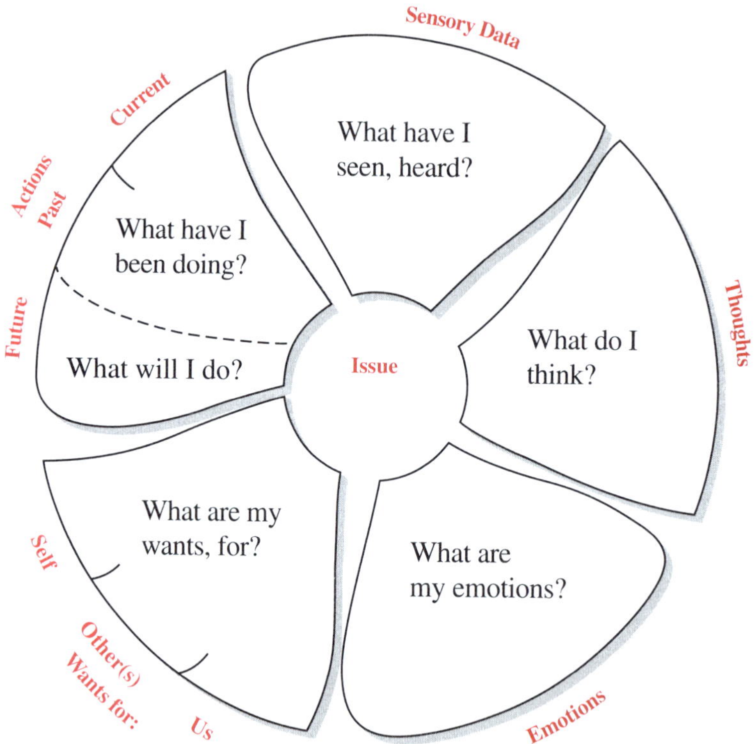

Resolving Your Issue

- As you systematically examine an issue, you may discover opposing information or parts that do not fit together comfortably (for example, a want that does not square with a thought or feeling). The Awareness Wheel guides you to the specifics of internal conflict that you must resolve to choose an effective future action — the next step.

- Note that you can experience the negative form of zones of the Awareness Wheel: "I did not see . . ."; "I don't think . . ."; "I'm not happy . . ."; "I do not want . . ."; or "I did not do . . ."

- To change the way you feel, consider re-examining or expanding your sensory data, altering your thinking, prioritizing your wants, or changing your behavior.

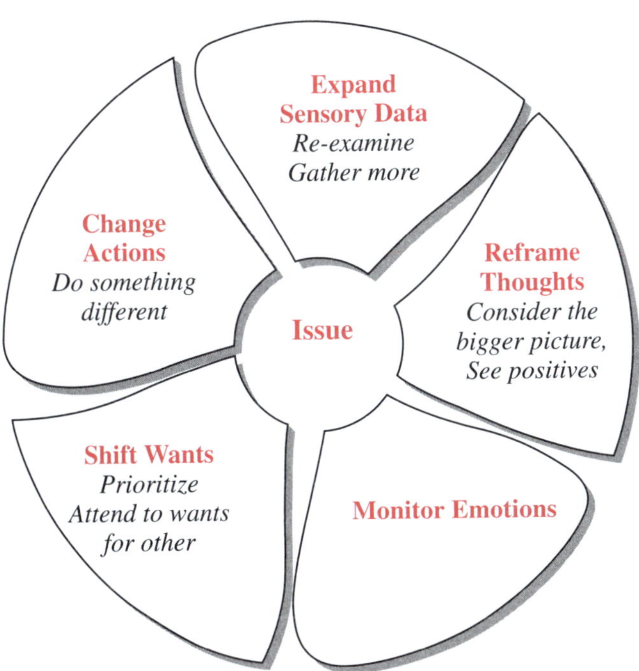

- Sometimes the issue you start with is not the real issue. Rather, in the process of expanding your awareness, you discover a deeper, more central or encompassing concern to be the major issue. Begin a new Wheel, putting this more central issue in the hub.

- Big issues usually require small next steps. If you wait until you think of a big solution, you may stay stuck. Start small.

- If an obvious next step (future action) does not emerge immediately, go around the Wheel again — take a deep breath, let yourself relax, and re-cycle the issue.

Like peeling an onion, this allows your deeper, less obvious (not conscious) thoughts, feelings, and wants to surface.

- When you come upon a solution, you will often experience a "felt shift" in your emotions from anxiety to peace or calm.

- If you do not find a clear next step or new awareness after recycling the Wheel a couple of times, set the issue (your Wheel) aside for a while. You may need additional time to reflect. Go on living, letting your current awareness interact ("cook") with new data and life experience. In the meanwhile, you can be confident that you have a tool to help you manage yourself and the issue as it unfolds.

- Sometimes you must involve your partner or other people, too, to resolve an issue. What the self-talk process does is heighten your awareness of your choices, including a difficult one. It provides a solid start.

- Using self-talk can make you a stronger, healthier person.

Points About Future Actions

- The key word for future action is "will": "I will do . . ."; "I will commit to . . . "

- Wanting — intending to do something — and thinking about what you could do are not the same as committing to a future action.

- Rather than a future action, sometimes understanding alone is the solution.

- Occasionally, failure to take a future action is simply avoidance of the issue.

INTUITION

Intuition is the experience of putting your Awareness Wheel together quickly and congruently (often not consciously). The Wheel also enables you to document the zones of your intuitions more specifically and share them with others more clearly.

SELF-TALK

Instructions

Huddle with your partner privately. Each of you choose a different issue —a topical or personal issue (not a relational issue with your partner) that both of you will be comfortable discussing in front of another couple (if you are in a group). The other couple will observe and help coach you as you process your issue using your Awareness Wheel skills floor mat. (Refer to your list of issues on page 42.)

Write the issue of your choosing in the hub of the Awareness Wheel below. Then, fill out your Wheel privately, in any order, using key words or phrases that represent your experience.

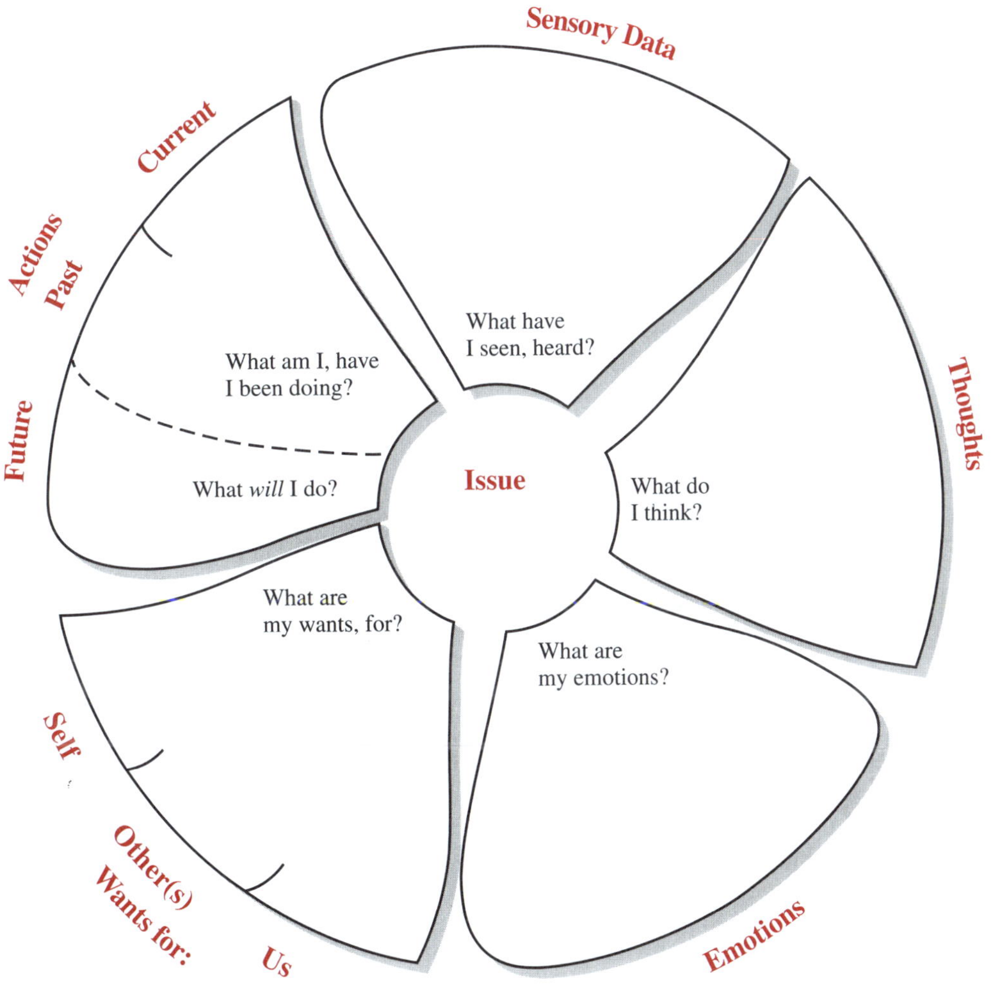

SIX TALKING SKILLS — for Aware Talk, Style IV

If you choose to share your self-information with someone else, six talking skills, based on the Awareness Wheel, will help you do so more clearly, directly, and completely. The six skills are:

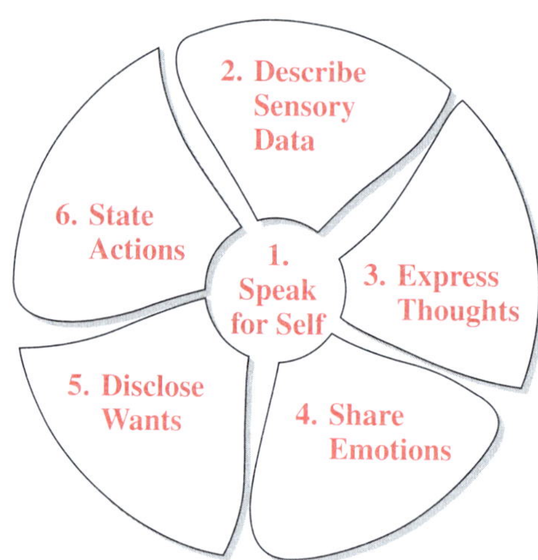

1. SPEAK FOR SELF (from my experience, perspective)

This skill is basic to all the other talking skills. It is critical to making your message more apt to be listened to and accepted rather than ignored and rejected.

To speak for yourself, combine a personal pronoun — I, me, my, or mine — with any zone(s) of your Awareness Wheel to form a message.

"I saw you smile when I mentioned watching a movie tonight."

"Here's my idea."

"Your response really pleases me."

"I'd like more time to think about it."

"I will check with the bank this afternoon."

Speaking for Self gives you a voice. It counts self by demonstrating:

- Uniqueness — my individuality and diversity
- Ownership — my responsibility and accountability
- Confidence — the legitimacy and validity of my perspective
- Authority — my acknowledgement and acceptance of my experience
- Assertion — my right to speak my own awareness

UNPRODUCTIVE ALTERNATIVES TO SPEAKING FOR SELF

Speak for Other(s) Over-Responsible	**Speak for Self** Self-Responsible	**Speak for No One** Under-Responsible

Makes:

You, We, They, or Everyone Statements

For example:

"You shouldn't do that." vs. "I'd like you to try doing that this way."

"Don't let that bother you."

"They know better."

"Everyone wants it."

Makes:

It, One, Some People, Other or Vague Reference Statements.

For example:

"It might be good to consider this." vs. "I'd like you to consider this."

"One could get upset about this."

"Some people don't care."

Speaking for Other(s):

- Superimposes your views on others
- "Boxes" other(s) in
- Generates defensiveness and resistance (simply by the way you say it)
- Is often invasive, intrusive
- Denies difference, uniqueness
- Discounts others

Speaking for No One:

- Speaks indirectly
- Diminishes your authority
- Suggests lack of confidence
- Avoids clarity (about who gives the message or what is meant)
- Is cautious, uncommitted
- Seems distant, often formal
- Devalues self

Benefits of Speaking for Self:

- Makes messages clearer and easier to hear
- Reduces defensiveness/resistance in others by not hemming them in
- Allows and encourages other views — differences, choices
- Values self, respects others

2. DESCRIBE SENSORY DATA

Describe what you see, hear, touch, taste, or smell — your observations (verbal and nonverbal):

- Supply specific who, what, where, when, and how information. Give concrete examples.

    "This morning, I heard Jack say he has a make-up game this weekend."

- Include pertinent facts, figures, and information from print and other sources.

    "I noticed the balance in our check book is down."

- The more descriptive, specific, and pertinent the information is, the stronger the data.

3. EXPRESS THOUGHTS

Say what you think — believe, interpret, expect, imagine to be possible.

    "I think we can find a place to live that will be closer to work for us both."

    "I believe that road will be closed for repairs."

Document

- Link interpretations to sensory data (observations). This lets others know how you have drawn your conclusions.

    "With only two days left, I don't think we are going to be ready to leave on our vacation."

    "I think my comment upset you. I noticed you got quiet."

4. SHARE EMOTIONS

Give your emotions directly.

- You can do so without using the word "feel." Simply say:

    "I'm thrilled about your promotion."

    "Waiting is frustrating for me."

    "I'm scared that I may have missed the deadline."

- Avoid using the common phrase, "I feel that . . . " This usually refers to a thought and does not clearly report an emotion.

- Directly identifying and giving words to emotions will help you:

    - Ground and discharge negative emotions effectively, freeing you to move on.

    - Add clarity to your communication.

5. DISCLOSE WANTS

Directly express your desires for **Self**, **Other(s)**, *and* **Us**.

> "I'd like to make a decision as soon as possible, for my own scheduling."

> "I don't want you to be pressured to decide too fast. I heard you say you need some time to think about it" (sensory data).

> "I want our vacation to be fun for both of us."

Note: Be sure to distinguish between wants *from* Other (from your partner, for you) and wants *for* Other (based on your partner's interests). This is essential for collaboration.

Disclosing Wants:

- Eliminates hidden agenda.
- Does not guarantee that you will get all your wants, but puts them on the table for negotiation.
- Builds relationship by acknowledging and engaging others' interests.

6. STATE ACTIONS

State what you have done, are doing, or will do.

> "My mind was somewhere else, and I really didn't hear what you said."

> "I agree with what you have just said."

> "I promise not to kid you about that again."

Owning your own behavior says you are:

- Aware
- Accountable (trustworthy)
- Responsible
- Committed

Recognize the difference between saying, "I might," "I could," or "I want to," and clearly committing yourself to Future Action, by saying "I will." Commitment to act distinguishes Skill # 6 (committed actions) from Skill # 5 (more tentative wants, wishes and desires).

USE THE TALKING SKILLS IN ANY ORDER

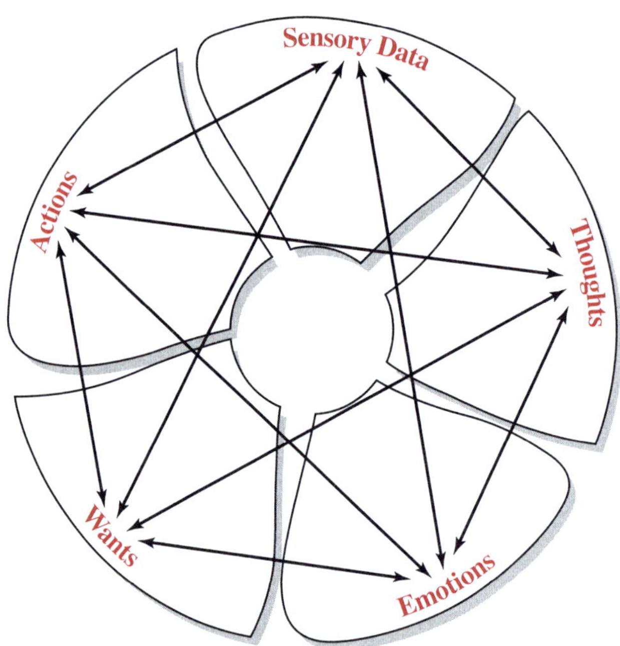

- The skills are numbered for convenient identification, not for use in a sequence. Apply them in any order as you share information about yourself.

- An effective message does not need to be lengthy. Use the talking skills to send multi-part messages — three or more zones of your Awareness Wheel in 30 seconds or less.

- A multi-part message is much clearer than a message that goes on and on in one zone.

COMMUNICATION STYLES AND TALKING SKILLS

Taking the "High Road"

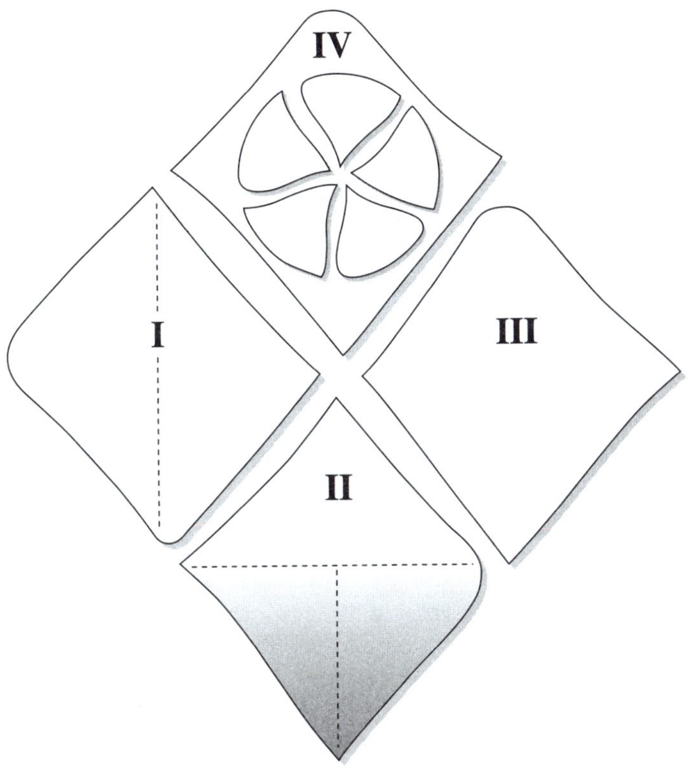

The Talking *Skills* correspond with the Talking *Styles*.

Consider the skills separately:

- Describing Sensory Data is associated with Small Talk and Shop Talk.
- Expressing Thoughts hovers in Search Talk.

Consider the skills combined:

- Sharing Emotions, Disclosing Wants, and Stating Actions are essential ingredients of Aware Talk.
- All the talking skills in combination support Aware Talk.

CARING ABOUT YOURSELF

Consider These Summary Points:

- Self-awareness is the most important resource you bring to any issue or situation.

- Self-awareness and self-disclosure are two different processes. Self-awareness is essential. Self-disclosure is a choice.

- The more parts of your Wheel you disclose, the clearer your message.

- Self-awareness increases self-control.

- You can use your Awareness Wheel to auger deeper, in order to reduce stress, manage tension, and resolve issues.

- Connecting with all parts of your experience integrates fragmented information and releases blocked energy, which helps generate constructive future actions.

- Partial awareness yields poor outcomes.

- Knowing yourself is not the same as being selfish and self-centered.

- Caring behavior, which matches your experience with congruent words and actions, creates energy, strength, and health.

- Wherever you go, you can use your Awareness Wheel. To use it, ask yourself, "What am I experiencing right now?"

Tips:

- Expand awareness before taking action.

- Increase your choices by gaining self-awareness.

- Ask yourself, "Are my actions (what I say and do) consistent with all parts of my Awareness Wheel?"

- To avoid giving mixed messages, consider your data, thoughts, feelings, wants and actions. Express them in Aware Talk.

> Each person's experience is unique, and each partner has his or her own separate awareness about a situation or issue.

 **Tools**

LEARNING AND APPLICATION TOOLS

The tools, which are part of your Couple Packet, can help you with practice for taking the high road during a conversation. They can assist you in learning and applying the COUPLE COMMUNICATION concepts, skills, and processes.

Awareness Wheel Pad

The Awareness Wheel pad has a number of uses. Suggestions include:

- Thinking through an issue alone (self-talk) by writing your experiences regarding the issue in the various zones.

- Preparing for an important conversation (with your partner or with another person) by filling out the zones that relate or that you want to cover. Remember, self awareness is essential. Disclosure is a choice.

- "Standing in your partner's shoes" — filling out an Awareness Wheel on what you believe your partner (or someone else) is experiencing (prior to having a conversation with that person).

Awareness Wheel Floor Mat

The Awareness Wheel floor mat can be applied in several ways in addition to its use in the class. These include:

- Thinking through an issue alone (self-talk) when you do not want to sit and write but would rather be up moving about.

- Rehearsing your part of an important, upcoming conversation with someone.

- Prompting the talking skills as you share your awareness about an issue with your partner.

Pocket Card Set

These cards are a quick reference and a prompt for your skill practice and application. Keep them where they are handy for you.

TALKING SKILLS ACTION PLAN

Instructions: Below is a list of the talking skills from Chapter 3. Complete the following steps:

Step 1. Without consulting your partner, mark each item twice: first with an "X" to represent your *current* use of each talking skill, and again with an "O" (circle) to represent your more-so or less-so *desired* use. If your *typical* and *desired* behaviors are the same, the "X" and "O" marks will be on the same number. If they are not the same, the marks will fall on different numbers.

When you are with your partner, how often do you:		**Seldom**					**Often**
1.	Speak for Self?	1	2	3	4	5	6
2.	Describe Sensory Data?	1	2	3	4	5	6
3.	Express Thoughts?	1	2	3	4	5	6
4.	Share Emotions?	1	2	3	4	5	6
5.	Disclose Wants for:						
	Self?	1	2	3	4	5	6
	Partner?	1	2	3	4	5	6
	Us?	1	2	3	4	5	6
6.	State Actions?	1	2	3	4	5	6

Step 2. Choose and list one or two skills to emphasize during practice between now and the next session.

Skill: _______________________________________

Skill: _______________________________________

Step 3. Compare your choices with your partner, and talk about where and when each of you will practice using the skills.

Between Sessions: When you notice your partner using the talking skill(s) he or she has chosen to practice between sessions, give your partner some positive feedback for using the skill(s). Encourage your partner by telling how the skill makes his or her messages clearer and increases your understanding (even if it is a difficult message to receive).

TALKING SKILLS IDENTIFICATION

Instructions: Each of the fifteen statements below combines the skill "speaking for self" with one of the five zones of the Awareness Wheel, resulting in one of the other talking skills. Identify the talking skill in each statement by placing the letter for the skill on the line provided.

a)   Describe Sensory Data

b)   Express Thoughts

c)   Share Emotions

d)   Disclose Wants

e)   State Actions

Answer

1. I'd like to set aside time to talk about our vacation next week.   _______
2. I get angry and frustrated when you say one thing and do another.   _______
3. I don't believe that is important.   _______
4. Wow, was I excited to hear that news!   _______
5. I expect a good report.   _______
6. I didn't make an appointment.   _______
7. I notice you're leaning back in your chair, smiling.   _______
8. I think you misunderstood her.   _______
9. I will call Tom tomorrow morning.   _______
10. I'm happy about that.   _______
11. I wish I would hear from him.   _______
12. I smell the food cooking.   _______
13. I hope to go there again.   _______
14. I'm reading a book now.   _______
15. I heard you say at lunch that you were interested in going with us.   _______

The answers are:

1.d, 2.c, 3.b, 4.c, 5.b, 6.e, 7.a, 8.b, 9.e, 10.c, 11.d, 12.a, 13.d, 14.e, 15.a

CHANGING FIGHT AND SPITE TALK TO AWARE TALK

Instructions: Each of the ten statements below is an example of Fight Talk or Spite Talk. Use the space between statements to change the message into Aware Talk.

1. "You never help around here, and I do it all. You're lazy."

2. "You're always late. Can't you ever be on time?"

3. "Don't be a jerk. Grow up."

4. "We'll just do what you say, since you're always right" (sarcastic tone).

5. "If I were as smart as you, I would have seen the mistake."

6. "You're too quiet in social situations. You look dumb."

7. "No, nothing's wrong. What makes you think that?"

8. "Nobody ever pays attention to me."

9. "You're selfish and inconsiderate."

Some possible Aware Talk statements for the sentences above include the following:

1. "I feel overwhelmed with so many chores, and I'd like some help. Would you be willing to help me?"
2. "I get frustrated and angry when you don't arrive at the time we agreed upon."
3. "Here's what I'd like to see, because I think it shows more responsibility."
4. "I don't agree with how you want us to do this. Can we talk about an alternative?"
5. "I didn't see the mistake."
6. "I feel uncomfortable when I think you're too quiet in social situations."
7. "Yes, I am upset. I think I'm being discounted."
8. "I wish we could talk together now."
9. "In this situation, I believe you are mainly thinking about yourself and not considering others. For instance, . . ."

BETWEEN-SESSION APPLICATIONS

Prepare and Share

In the upcoming week, set aside some time with your partner to tell him or her about something of importance to you. (If it would be helpful, look at your list of issues from the THRIVE Sphere or from page 42 in this workbook.)

Ahead of time, use either the Awareness Wheel pad or mat to prepare. During the conversation, use the mat to prompt your use of the talking skills as you share your awareness.

Apply Scripture

Return to the scriptures at the front of this chapter. Review and reflect on the verses in relation to your own awareness and disclosure. In what ways do the skills you have learned from this chapter help you apply the scripture verses on talking?

Find a time for you and your partner to converse about the insights.

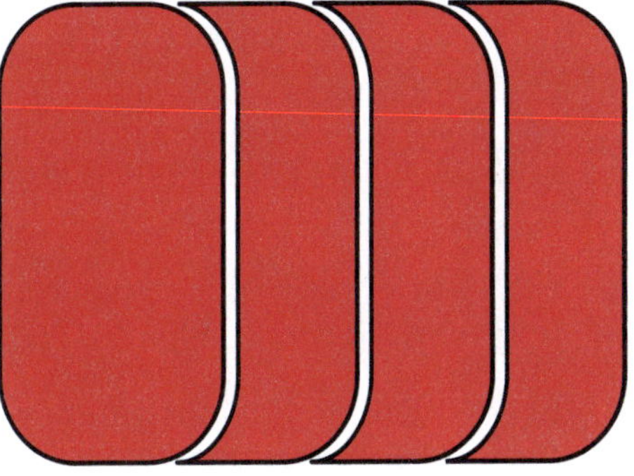

CHAPTER 4

Consider how the scriptures, and especially those from Proverbs, refer to listening and gaining understanding:

Everyone should be quick to listen, slow to speak, and slow to become angry. *James 1:9b*

He who answers before listening — that is his folly and his shame. The heart of the discerning acquires knowledge; the ears of the wise seek it out. *Proverbs 18:13 and 18:15*

The purposes of a man's heart are deep waters, but a man of understanding draws them out. *Proverbs 20:5*

How much better to get wisdom than gold, to choose understanding rather than silver. *Proverbs 16:16*

He who listens to a life-giving rebuke will be at home among the wise. *Proverbs 15:31*

The way of a fool seems right to him, but a wise man listens to advice. *Proverbs 12:15*

He who cherishes understanding prospers. Listen to advice and accept instruction, and in the end you will be wise. *Proverbs 19:8b and 19:20*

Blessed is the man who finds wisdom, the man who gains understanding. *Proverbs 3:13*

4

APPLYING THE LISTENING CYCLE

Styles of Listening
Listening Cycle Map
5 Listening Skills

In the same way that self awareness is important for clearer communication between you and your partner, so is understanding him or her well, especially when you have a serious conversation. Effective listening is the key to that understanding.

Many times listening is simply a way to connect with and enjoy your partner. At other times, listening concerns a decision or disagreement that arises between you. In these cases, how you listen takes on greater significance. For building and maintaining a collaborative relationship, listening skills become essential tools.

This chapter describes styles of listening characteristic of, or appropriate for, various situations and then provides specific skills for times when deep listening is required.

> Different styles of listening create corresponding levels
> of information, trust, and intimacy.

STYLES OF LISTENING

Your style of listening — how you listen — determines the quality of information the other person shares. The key to effective listening is to manage yourself by using a listening style that fits the situation.

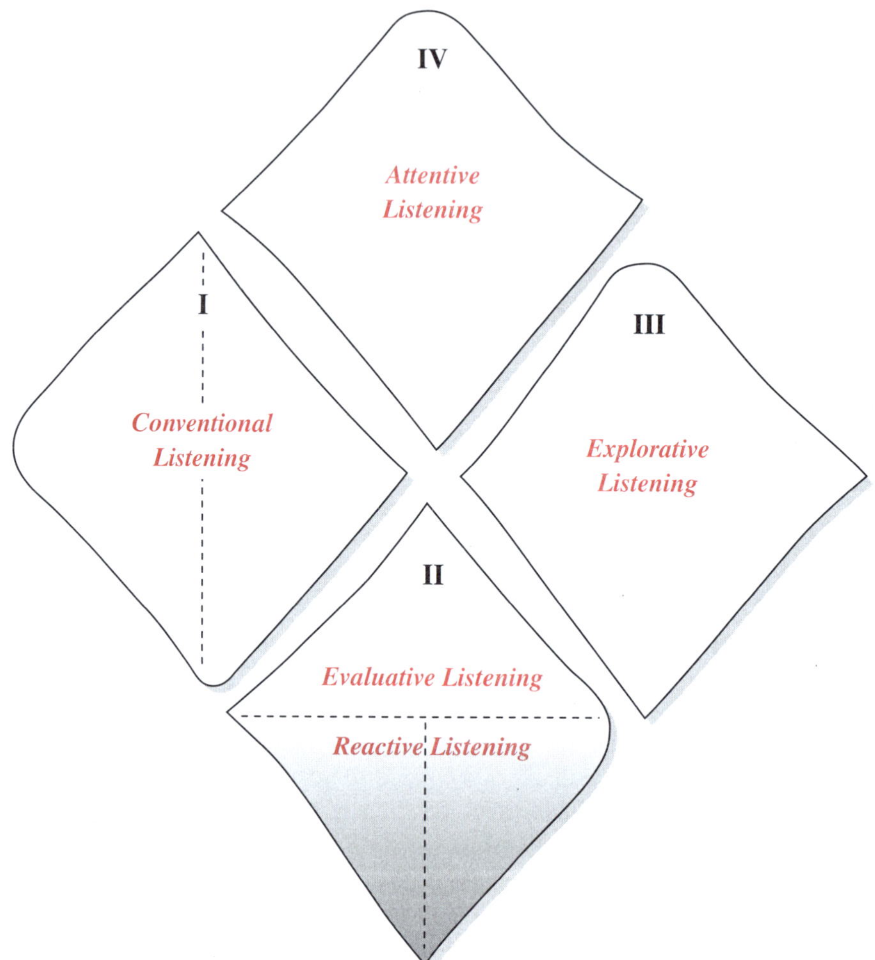

Different Situations Call for Different Listening Styles

- Style I — Conventional Listening takes in day-to-day information.
- Style II — Evaluative Listening judges information and can lead easily into a Reactive, defensive mode.
- Style III — Explorative Listening uses questions to probe for information.
- Style IV — Attentive Listening takes you to the heart of the matter.

Most of this chapter focuses on the listening skills associated with Styles III and IV— Explorative and Attentive Listening — the two best styles for listening to understand each other. These styles help you share confidences and resolve important, complicated, or conflicted issues collaboratively — to take the high road when it really counts.

Styles I and II — Conventional and Evaluative/Reactive Listening — common ways of listening, yield different results.

STYLE I — CONVENTIONAL LISTENING

Conventional Listening is the way you typically show interest in Small Talk or Shop Talk. You connect and make yourself available in a pleasant, sociable way.

Behaviors of Style I

In Conventional Listening, you:

- Serve as a relaxed sounding board for chit-chat and stories.
- Ask questions of a general nature to keep the exchange going.
- Respond non-verbally on a light level to stay connected.
- Gather information.
- Begin to listen half-heartedly to signal your wish to shift the conversation to something more substantial, or to exit the conversation.

Associational Listening

When a talker's conversation reminds you (the listener) of a similar situation, topic, or experience, you shift the conversation to talking about your own experience. This can have a positive or negative impact. For example, it is:

- Positive, when everyone joins in, trading stories, laughing and enjoying each other's contribution, which energizes and keeps a conversation going.
- Negative, when it becomes a take-away — a disruption or distraction from the other person's point or story. This is particularly true when the other person is trying to say something serious and important to him or her.

Impact of Conventional Listening

This listening style:

- Contributes to a relaxing, enjoyable time together.
- Keeps a conversation going about fascinating or routine matters.

- Can trigger annoyance if the talker wants a deeper response.
- Is less conducive to discovering critical information.

STYLE II — EVALUATIVE AND REACTIVE LISTENING

In this style, you listen in a way that tries to control the path of the conversation. As you do so, you take an evaluative stance, listening to hear if the other person discloses information that is useful or not to you, or with which you agree or disagree. While the intensity of your evaluating can vary, your behavior often becomes anxious and defensive, and then you slide easily into being reactive. You attempt to squelch and counter information that does not fit your point of view.

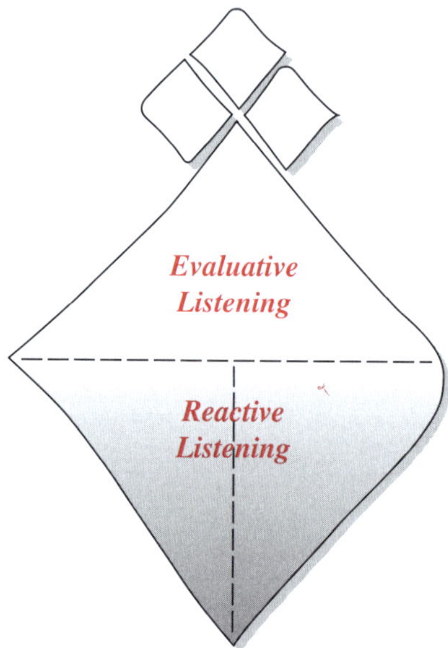

Examples of Evaluative and Reactive Listening Behaviors:

Judging, such as: "That's right, wrong, good, bad, smart, foolish."

Internally rehearsing a rebuttal

Interrupting with statements or challenging questions to take over the conversation and dispute a point

Listening selectively, disattending to, ignoring critical information

Assuming, mind-reading, projecting (your experience on other)

Asking questions to cover your own hidden agenda: "Don't you think. . . ?"

Using "Why" questions that call for justification and imply blame

Interrogating: "Tell me what you're thinking. Speak up!"

Crowding (aggressive) or *disengaging* (distancing) *gestures when the other is talking*

Ignoring, twisting, distorting, or manipulating what the talker says in an attempt to force agreement or change

Impact of Evaluative and Reactive Listening

On the positive side, this listening style can energize an exchange and even stimulate action. For example, when time is short and a quick decision must be made, you listen long enough to get information significant to you, and then take control. As you do so, others go along with you.

More often however, its impact is negative, especially when someone is trying to explain his or her side of things. In these cases, the listening style is inefficient and generates anger and frustration, yielding unsatisfactory results. Disagreements quickly become power struggles rather than information exchanges (with anyone involved vying for who is right or wrong). Lack of listening skills leaves people stuck.

Typically, the style:

- Shows an attitude of discounting the talker — "I count, you don't."

- Signals resistance.

- Generates stress — tension, frustration, anger, and defensiveness.

- Undermines rapport and trust.

- Spawns fragmented, inaccurate, and misleading information.

- Prolongs the resolution process and results in poor decisions.

- Runs the risk of creating bad feelings and of damaging relationships.

When you listen evaluatively and reactively, you keep yourself front and center, focusing attention more on your own experience rather than on the other person's.

> Am I really listening or
> just anxiously waiting to talk?

STYLE III — EXPLORATIVE LISTENING

Explorative Listening is a style used to search for and increase significant information regarding complex or non-routine issues and situations. Through the use of questions, this style develops perspective.

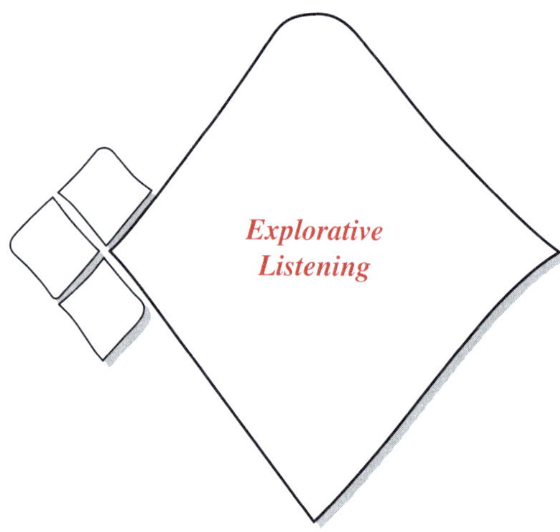

Explorative Listening Behaviors

In this style, questions are used for:

Getting a conversation started

Influencing/Guiding the conversation

Probing for information in a non-accusatory fashion

Gaining/Expanding information or perspective

Filling in missing or unclear parts of the Awareness Wheel

Clarifying misunderstandings

Clearing up confusion

Confirming information

Generating possibilities

Seeking advice

Making Requests

"Testing the water"

Types of Questions

The structure of a question limits or expands the kind and quality of information disclosed by the talker. One form generates either-or kinds of answers. The other form elicits broader or more widely extended, open-ended kinds of answers, and this form is referred to as an open question.

Either-Or Questions

Questions that begin with a "being verb" — is, are, do, was, did, has, have, could, would, will — stimulate an either-or answer. Often the questions call for a "Yes" or "No" answer, though other types of either-or answers occur, as well. For example:

"Is there enough gas in the car?" (yes or no)

"Are you pleased?" (yes or no)

"Will you come home or stop at the store?" (home or store)

While either-or questions are efficient, they also narrow information. They are most often used in Conventional Listening with Small Talk and Shop Talk.

Open Questions

By adding "Who," "What," "Where," "When," or "How," to a "being verb," you create an "open question." Open questions have the potential of gaining more information.

For example:

"Who was at their house?" or "Where is it?"(data zone)

"What do you think about that?"(thought zone)

"How are you feeling about the decision?" (emotion zone)

"When would you like to go?" (want zone)

"What will you do?" (action zone)

Caution

Notice that "Why" is not included. Although "Why" is a good research question, it is often used to blame or demand justification (Reactive Listening). On the other hand, questions beginning with "Who," "What," "Where," "When," and "How," gain information about "Why" without the negative implications.

Tone also influences the response. If you use a negative tone, you can easily turn an open question into a reactive challenge.

Use The Awareness Wheel to Guide Open Questions

Most people ask questions (probe) randomly, hoping to tap into a useful piece of information that will be helpful. They have no map to guide their questioning. Besides being a map for talking, the Awareness Wheel is also a listening map, a guide for you to gain useful information effectively. The map will help you organize information, as well as fill in missing information.

To form a focused open question, combine "Who," "What," "Where," "When," and "How," (but not "Why") with any zone of the Awareness Wheel.

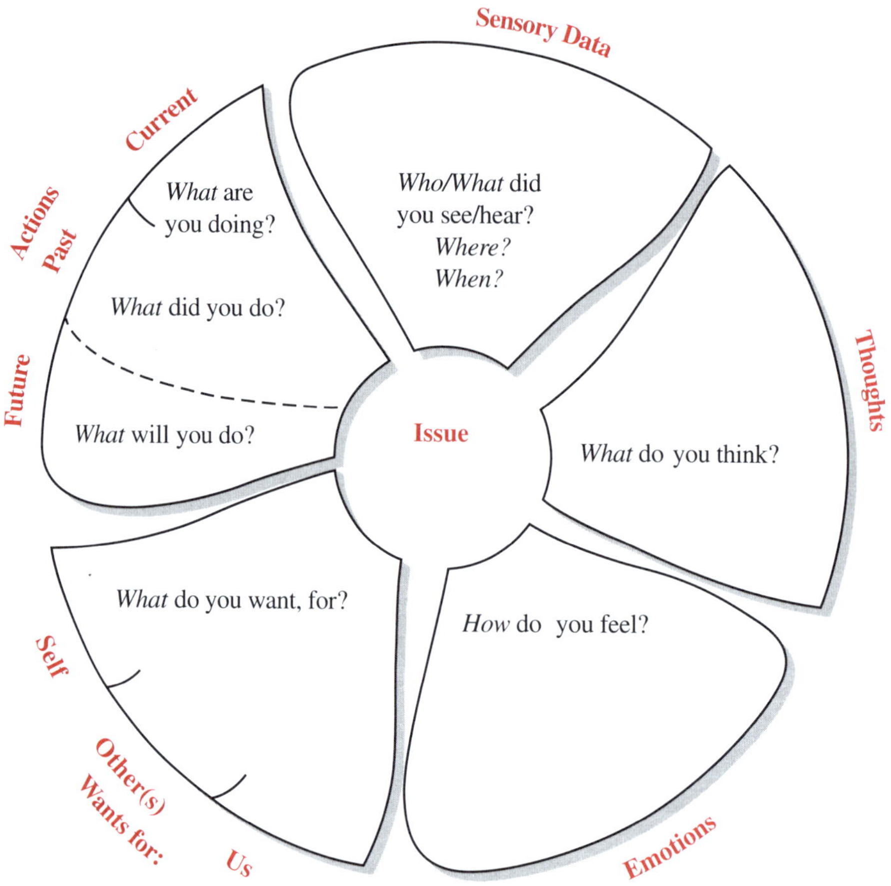

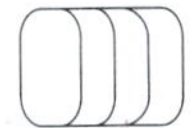

Special Use of Explorative Listening

Open questions are particularly useful in guiding a conversation with people who:

Talk *too little* — need prompting to tell their story completely.

Talk *too much* — need organization to help them focus.

Positive Impacts of Explorative Listening Using Open Questions

Open questions focus the conversation. They are used frequently to facilitate:

- Brainstorming
- Decision-making
- Issue exploration
- Problem solving
- Conflict resolution

Negative Impacts of Asking Questions, Even Open Questions

Questions, intentionally or unintentionally, run the risk of:

- Disrupting the spontaneous flow of a talker's story.
- Leading the conversation away from critical information.
- Shifting the focus from the talker's source experience to the listener's interests (agenda) or experience.
- Anticipating the next questions, rather than attending to immediate data.

Notice — All Questions Lead

As a listener asks questions to gain information, knowingly or unknowingly, he or she directs and influences — leads — the conversation. Since questions come out of the asker's mind (experience and agenda) and not necessarily from that of the responder, all questions lead. This may or may not be helpful. Be aware that questions can unintentionally (or intentionally) mis-direct or pre-close a conversation and get in the way of discovering critical information.

Put Questions To Good Use — Do Not Let Them Get In The Way

- *Think about when to ask questions.* People often ask questions too early and too much in a listening situation. (Many people think listening means solving problems, so their job as a listener is to guide the talker to a solution, or come up with the answer. As a result, they over direct or easily lapse into giving advice.)

- *Consider the necessity for questions.* Some people believe that they show their interest in a problem by taking over the conversation with questions. As a result, they often frustrate the talker

Points About Questions (Whether Either-Or or Open Questions)

- *Questions tend to limit the information given to that which is requested.* This can create the situation later in which the listener asks (blaming), "Why didn't you tell me that earlier?" The talker replies (also blaming), "I don't know. You never asked me."

- *Questions can place too much responsibility on the listener,* rather than allowing the talker to lead the listener to key information.

- *The value of a question is determined by the quality of information it produces.*

Explorative Listening using questions helps guide and focus information.

EXERCISE: ASKING OPEN QUESTIONS

Instructions

For questioner: Use Open Questions to fill out an Awareness Wheel on an issue of importance to your partner. Use the Wheel (below) as a guide for asking the questions and making notes as you fill out his or her experience.

For observers: As you observe the conversation, use a sheet from your Awareness Wheel pad to record your observations.

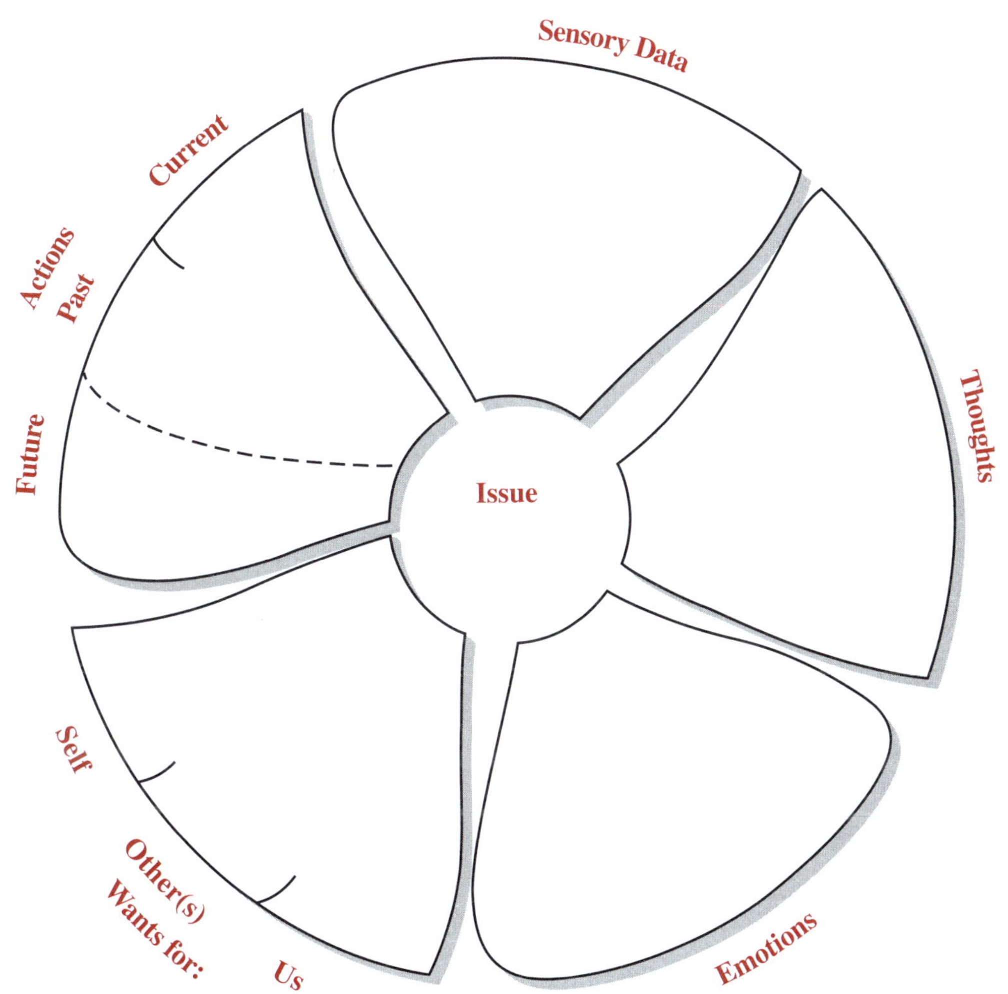

LISTENING PROCESSES

In an important conversation, many people listen only to agree or disagree with what they hear (rather than to understand what they hear prior to agreeing or disagreeing with it). They get caught in listening styles that limit the availability of content critical to the situation, and they do so by screening everything through their lens of agreement or disagreement. Discussions turn quickly into power struggles for control of who is right or who is wrong The exchange mainly increases their own and the other person's frustration and stress.

When it comes to listening, you have two questions to consider:

- Am I leading (trying to take charge), or am I following the other person's lead?

- Am I listening for agreement/disagreement, or am I listening for understanding?

Listening Intentions:

	To Agree/Disagree	**To Understand**
Leading	*Reactive Listening*	*Explorative Listening*
Following	*Evaluative Listening*	*Attentive Listening*

Listening Behaviors:

Reactive Listening and Evaluative Listening (Style II) listen strictly for agreement or disagreement. Reactive Listening *leads* (or attempts to) by forcefully accepting (agreeing) or rejecting (disagreeing). Evaluative Listening *follows* to judge. Whether intentional or not, these processes suppress or limit information.

Explorative Listening (Style III) seeks understanding, yet does so by *leading* through questioning. Because questions lead, they either discover or miss information.

Attentive Listening (Style IV) pursues understanding by *following*. This style enables the talker to lead the listener into greater understanding, without the listener agreeing or disagreeing. It encourages, rather than limits information. It gains the richest content, reduces stress, and strengthens relationship.

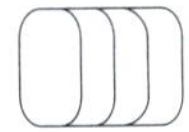

STYLE IV — ATTENTIVE LISTENING

Attentive Listening engages the talker, encouraging him or her to speak freely and fully about his or her experience. This style of listening fosters the flow and quality of information without the listener agreeing, disagreeing, or directing the conversation.

The Goal: To Understand

To reach understanding, you seek to:

- *Hear* in an uncontaminated way, your partner's (or another person's) "story."

- *Comprehend* his or her experience accurately.

- *Discover* useful information.

When you listen attentively, your awareness of your partner increases, typically resulting in information that is essential for building agreements as you negotiate, make decisions, or resolve conflicts. In the process, you demonstrate an "I-care-about-you" attitude, which often allows you to connect at a deeper level.

THE LISTENING CYCLE MAP: 5 SKILLS

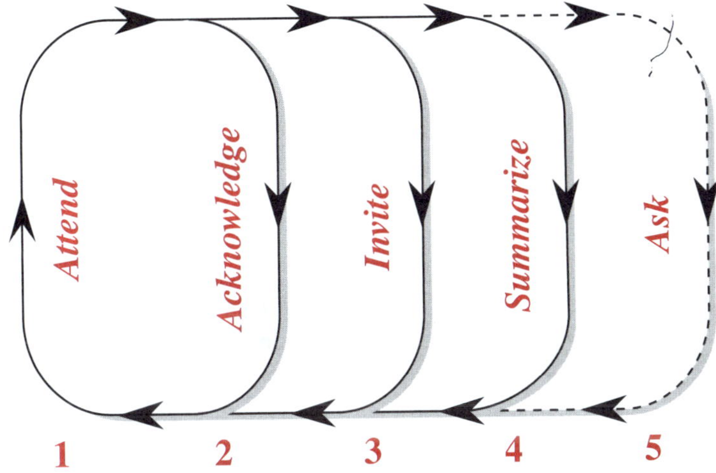

The Listening Cycle is a map of listening skills, providing a guide for applying the skills. With its use, you can maximize your ability to listen for understanding.

The first four skills of The Listening Cycle make up Attentive Listening — following skills. (The fifth skill of Asking Open Questions is the mainstay of the Explorative Listening Style, presented earlier in this chapter.) The following pages describe how to use the four skills.

ATTENTIVE LISTENING SKILLS

1. ATTEND — Look, Listen, Track

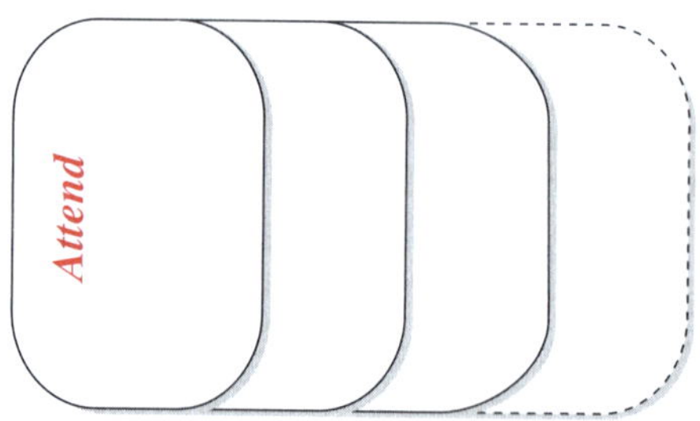

Attending means *following* the talker, *paying complete attention* (not multi-tasking — internally or externally), *being fully present* to his or her experience. This is a foundational listening skill.

As you listen with an open, inviting body posture, you allow yourself to sense the other's non-verbal emotional signals (mainly in his or her face), as well as to the words being spoken. As you synchronize with your partner, you gain emotional understanding — a connection called empathy — as well as an intellectual understanding of his or her thoughts, feelings and wants.

How to Attend:

- *Observe* the talker's nonverbals — shifts in posture, facial expression, tension and energy.
- *Listen* to the sounds of the voice — tone, pitch, pace, and volume of speech.
- *Track* the talker's Awareness Wheel — the content of what he or she says in terms of the zones of the Wheel. (See the graphic on the next page.)

Attending Tips

- Set your own concerns aside temporarily.
- Stop other activity that is, or could appear to be, distracting.
- Mirror the talker (sit/sit; stand/stand).
- Make eye contact as you listen.
- Let the talker set the pace (be the leader of the conversation). This signals your availability, receptivity, and interest.

To Track:

Follow what the talker says according to the zones of the Awareness Wheel.

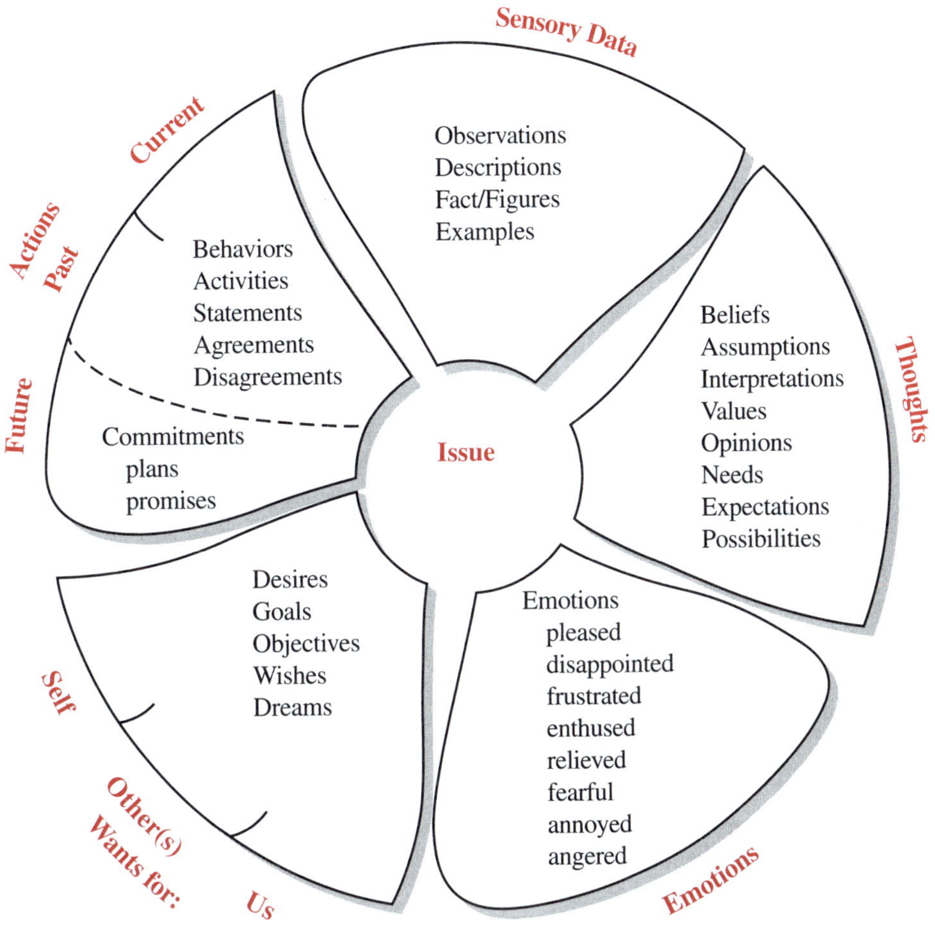

The Awareness Wheel will give you a map to follow (track) the content of a conversation. As you track:

- Notice the zones covered and those not addressed.

- Watch for congruence/incongruence — the match between the person's words and his or her nonverbals. (For example, your partner says, "I'm pleased" and looks pleased; or says, "I'm happy" but looks or sounds disappointed.)

Later you can ask open questions to fill in missing zones. Or you can disclose your own experience in a particular zone.

2. ACKNOWLEDGE — Other's Experience

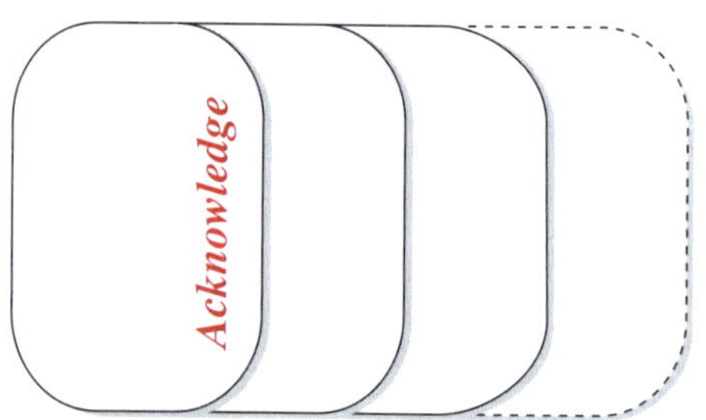

Acknowledgements are distillations — one or two words or a brief phrase — that you speak while the other person is talking, which capture accurately what he or she is saying and expressing nonverbally. For example:

"Challenging."

"New Opportunity."

"Frustrating."

How to Acknowledge

"Voice over" accurately, by coming in micro-seconds *behind* (following) the talker; *not ahead* (leading), which would be putting words into his or her mouth.

Acknowledging Tips

- Go beyond your nonverbal supportive facial expressions and sounds to verbalize explicitly what the talker is expressing.

- Move to where the talker is — data, thoughts, emotions, wants, actions — rather than where your urges are as a listener.

- Do not wait for the talker to pause, rather verbalize as the talker speaks. (When done well, these acknowledgements do not disrupt the talker but rather energize him or her. They act like sonar, confirming that you are on target. If you are off course, the talker will correct or calibrate your understanding.)

- Tune into your partner's experience and do not superimpose (project) your experience on him or her.

- Watch the talker's face for small nonverbals, such as nods and smiles or frowns and blank stares. They will signal the accuracy (or inaccuracy) of your understanding. When you touch the right chord, the talker will be energized. If you are off track, you will see it in his or her facial expressions and other nonverbals.

- Listen carefully and express unstated *feelings* and *wants*:

  Sore spots — anger, frustration (negative energy)

  Soft spots — fear, hurt, vulnerability

  Unfulfilled wants

  Blocked desires

  Hot spots — excitement

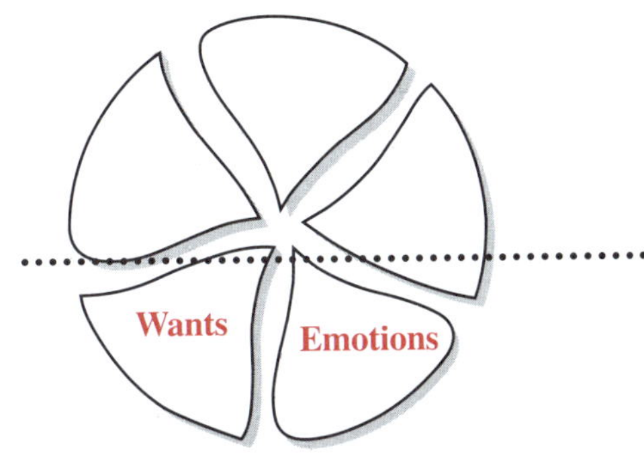

When You Acknowledge Your Partner, You:

- Show respect for and acceptance of his or her experience as being valid and legitimate for him or her. (This does not necessarily mean you agree. Your experience may be totally different.)

- Deepen connection with, and comprehension of, your partner's experience.

- Demonstrate that your partner has your moment-to-moment full attention and understanding.

Points About the Skill of Acknowledging

- Acknowledging confirms that you are following the other's story, and not sidetracking him or her with your concerns. You stand in the talker's shoes.

- Acknowledgements reduce the talker's anxiety by your offering no resistance.

- Acknowledging what the other person is experiencing, independent of whether you agree or disagree, is powerful. It is often all that is necessary to connect and create understanding.

- Attending and acknowledging build bridges. They show you care about the person, particularly important when this is your partner, and you affirm his or her right to talk and be understood. These skills are strong forces for building relationship and collaboration.

3. INVITE — More Information

Inviting means that *you say or do something that encourages the talker to continue spontaneously talking about whatever it is he or she wants to tell you.* The effect of an invitation is that the talker, not the listener, chooses where to go next.

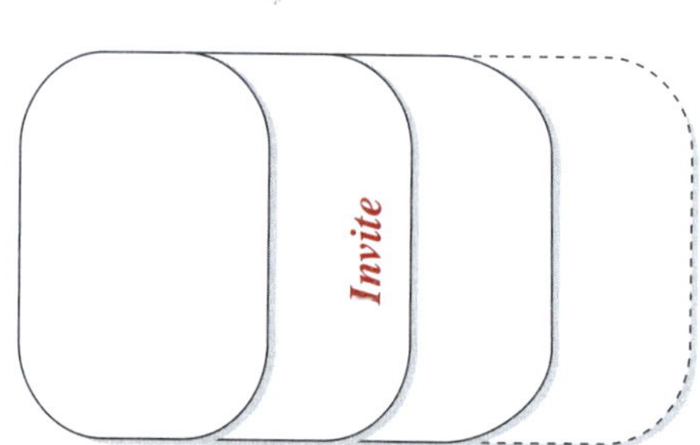

How to Invite:

- Inviting can take three forms:

    Gentle command:

    > "Continue."

    > "Say more."

    Wide Open Question (This does not focus on a specific zone of the Wheel.):

    > "What else?"

    > "Anything more?"

    Statement:

    > "I'd like to hear more."

    > "This is hard for me to hear, but I'd like you to continue."

Invite when:

- There is a pause.
- You experience the urge to react, disagree, or advise.
- You want to ask a question.

Keep inviting — Two, Three, or More Times:

- You will receive richer, more complete information.
- Continue inviting until the talker says he or she has nothing more to add. At that point you know the story is complete, and that it is time for a summary (the next

skill to be described) or for you to begin asking questions or talk yourself.

- Sometimes the talker will say he or she has nothing more to add, or will pause and go on to say, "But," and then give you a piece of informational gold.

Points About the Skill of Inviting

- Giving your partner maximum choice and freedom to tell his or her side of things usually produces the richest information, most efficiently.

- Inviting is a particularly useful skill when your partner wants to tell his or her experience, but for various reasons, you are prone to direct or take over for him or her.

- Inviting, like peeling an onion a layer at a time, will take you deeper into the core of your partner's experience.

- Essentially, each time you invite, you let your partner know, "What you are saying is important to me. I have time to listen. I want you to keep talking." As a result, most talkers relax, trust grows, and the person is more likely to tell you what is really going on — what he or she really thinks, feels, or wants.

- Typically, after receiving several invitations, the talker reveals information not yet said but important to the issue.

- Rather than playing a guessing game with questions, inviting lets your partner lead you to the critical information. Until he or she has no more to add, questions are premature and mainly distract and sidetrack.

- Inviting operationalizes the 80/20 rule. As a listener, you encourage and allow your partner to connect with his or her own uncontaminated experience regarding an issue or situation.

> Quality listening means getting the whole story accurately, the first time.

4. SUMMARIZE — to Ensure Accuracy

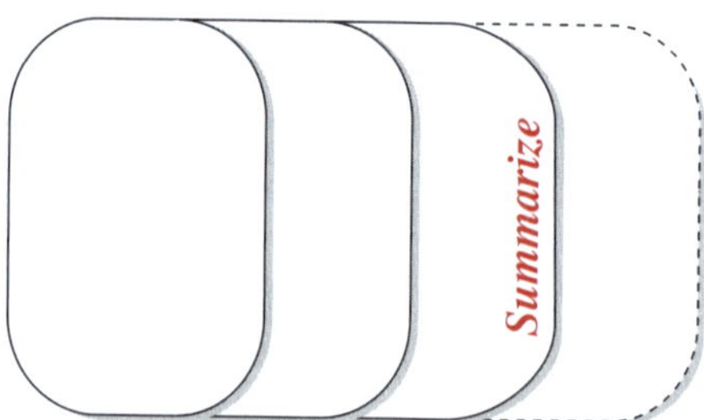

Summarizing means condensing a talker's message accurately. This demonstrates to the talker that you have understood accurately what he or she has said. It ensures that the message sent has been the message received, whether or not you agree with what the other has said.

How to Summarize:

- Condense in your own words what you have just heard to be the other person's points. It is often helpful to introduce your summary by stating, for example:

    "Let me see if I've got what you just said."

    "I'd like to run back what you've just told me to be sure I've got it."

- *Do not add to* (make inferences about) *or miss* important elements from the original message.

- Watch the talker's facial expression, such as nodding, smiling, or displaying other positive nonverbals, for a signal of accuracy.

- Ask for confirmation or clarification of your summary if the talker's response is unclear, uncertain, or disconfirming.

- Re-cycle a summary more than once until both of you are satisfied that the message received is an accurate, though condensed, representation of the message sent.

When to Summarize

It is useful to summarize at any point in a conversation when you:

Have an important issue at hand and believe understanding is critical

Think misunderstanding seems to be occurring

Experience a stressful exchange

Want to prioritize issues

Want to clarify perspectives

Want to resolve conflicts

Confirm an action plan

Points About the Skill of Summarizing

- People like to be heard accurately. Summarizing builds confidence, trust, and relationship.
- Interrupting someone to summarize his or her points is rarely seen as rude. Usually, quite the opposite, it is considered respectful.
- Summarizing punctuates a complicated conversation, assuring understanding before proceeding.
- A talker can ask the listener for a summary as well, without waiting for the listener to initiate one. ("Can you tell me what you've heard me say?")

Tip

Avoid saying, "I understand what you mean." (The statement is often used to take charge of or control a conversation, without real understanding.) Rather, demonstrate your understanding with an accurate summary.

5. ASK — Open Questions

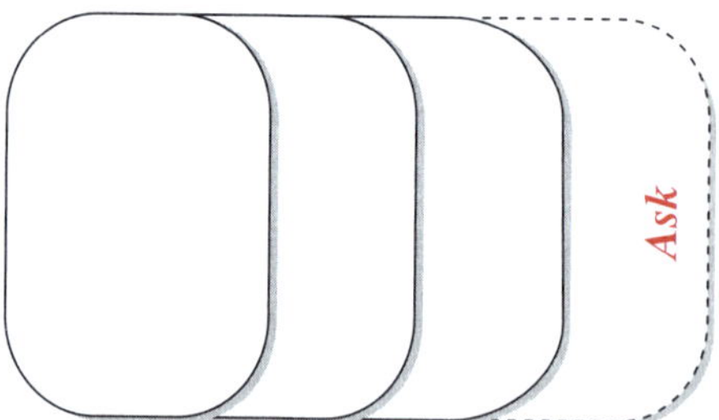

After you have helped a person tell you his or her concern or story as completely as possible using the Attentive Listening Skills 1 to 4 (described above), you may want to fill in missing information or clarify confusing parts. To do this, ask the open explorative questions of "Who," "What," "Where," "When," and "How." Consider asking questions from all the zones of the Awareness Wheel. For instance:

"Who was there?"

"What do you want for Jim (based on his interests)?"

"Where do you think this will take place?"

"How did you feel?"

"When are you going?"

- Remember, all questions lead! The dotted line in the Listening Cycle around "Ask" means use questions wisely.

- The better you get at Attentive Listening, the less you need to ask questions. Most people will take you more quickly to the heart of critical information if you let them guide you.

- Questions are helpful when you want to guide, structure, or limit information. Usually though, if given the chance, most people tell their story best with acknowledgements and invitations rather than with probing questions.

APPLY THE LISTENING CYCLE

Listening for understanding (distinct from listening for agreement or disagreement) is a learned behavior. It does not come naturally. The Listening Cycle can help you listen for understanding.

The Listening Cycle guides and combines the skills for most effective listening. While each of the five skills can be used independently and in any order as you listen, you heighten your ability to understand another by combining the skills to continue following the talker. This is especially significant when you are discussing a *complex* or *stressful* issue.

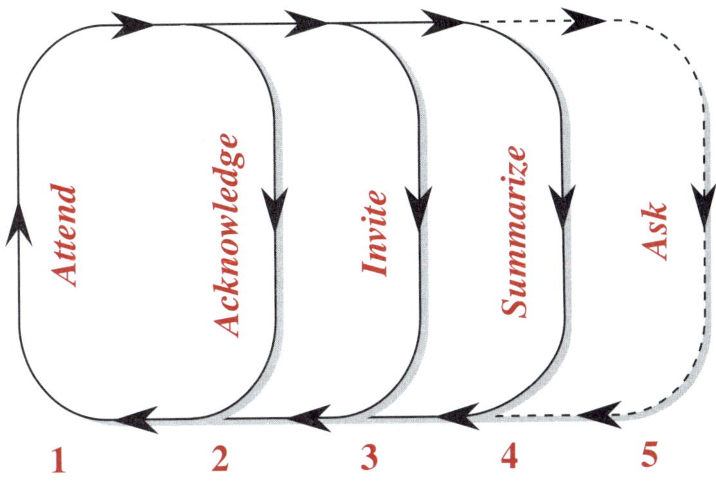

- Notice in the Listening Cycle, the solid lines that circulate among the Attentive Listening skills —Attend, Acknowledge, Invite, and Summarize. Recycling these skills, in any order, produces the highest quality of useable information possible.

- Ask (open questions) is positioned last and set off by dotted lines. This is to remind you to use questions wisely. The better you become at using the first four listening skills, the less you need to rely on questions.

- Two skill combinations that are particularly useful when used in sequence are:

    Acknowledge and Invite

    Summarize and Invite

Points About Listening

- Some people fear that the actual process of listening for understanding will be read by the talker as agreement, when in fact the listener is not in agreement. If this becomes a concern during a conversation, simply clarify that you are not in agreement but that you are trying to understand accurately the talker's perspective. (Then invite the talker to continue.)

- The Attentive Listening skills do not all have to be used together and at one time. More often, the skills are used separately and sprinkled throughout a conversation.

- Not all situations call for complete and full understanding. Use Styles of Listening flexibly.

- Being pre-occupied, self-absorbed, or feeling anxious interferes with the ability to listen for understanding.

- A big difference exists between partners who can listen to each other for understanding and a couple who cannot. The latter are stuck listening only for agreement or disagreement.

Natural Behaviors:	Learned Skills:
Ignore	Attend
Interrupt	Acknowledge
Talk or Question	Invite
Assume	Summarize
Tell	Ask

CARING ABOUT YOUR PARTNER

When you use the Listening Cycle, you set your own concerns aside temporarily as you allow and encourage your partner to express his or her experience fully. In the process, you demonstrate care for him or her.

Positive outcomes and benefits for your partner include:

- Getting to the center of an issue faster with less interpersonal stress.
- Receiving support to discover and share his or her own critical information.
- Being understood.
- Developing, in many cases, a solution to his or her concern.
- Increasing choices and influence.
- Enjoying a collaborative atmosphere.
- Feeling good about you, which develops trust and builds relationship.

> Attentive Listening is a non-material gift you can give
> to your partner on a regular basis.

CARING ABOUT YOURSELF ALSO

When you listen attentively to your partner, besides demonstrating care for him or her, you also express care for yourself.

Some of the same positive outcomes and benefits for your partner come to you, as well. These include:

- Getting to the center of an issue faster with less interpersonal stress.
- Enjoying a collaborative atmosphere.
- Feeling good about your own part in connecting, which develops trust and builds relationship.

In addition:

- Typically, your partner is willing to listen to you, since you have first listened to him or her.

MY LISTENING STYLES

Instructions

Step 1. Think of the listening styles you use when you are conversing with your partner. Estimate the percentage of time you *typically* spend in each of the styles. Then, if you would like to change how you listen with your partner, put a plus (+) in the style(s) you want to increase and a minus (—) in the ones you want to decrease.

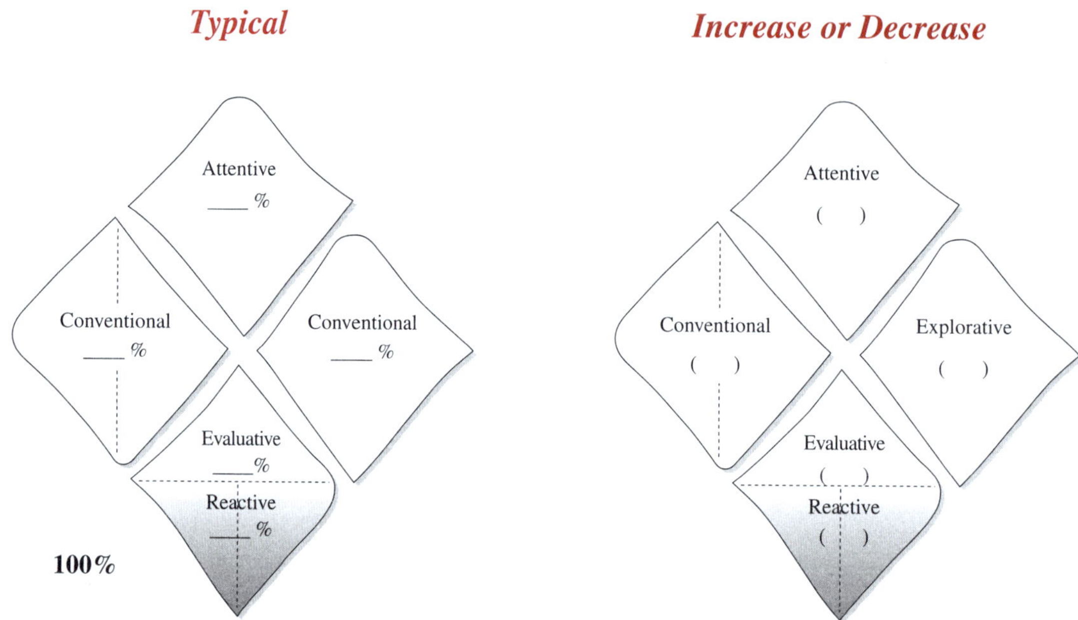

Step 2. Complete the worksheet on the next page, "My Partner's Listening Styles."

MY PARTNER'S LISTENING STYLES

Instructions

Step 2 continued. Think of the listening styles your partner uses when he or she is conversing with you. Estimate the percentage of time he or she *typically* spends in each of the styles. If you would like your partner to alter his or her listening style, put a plus (+) in the style(s) you want increased and a minus (—) in the ones you want decreased.

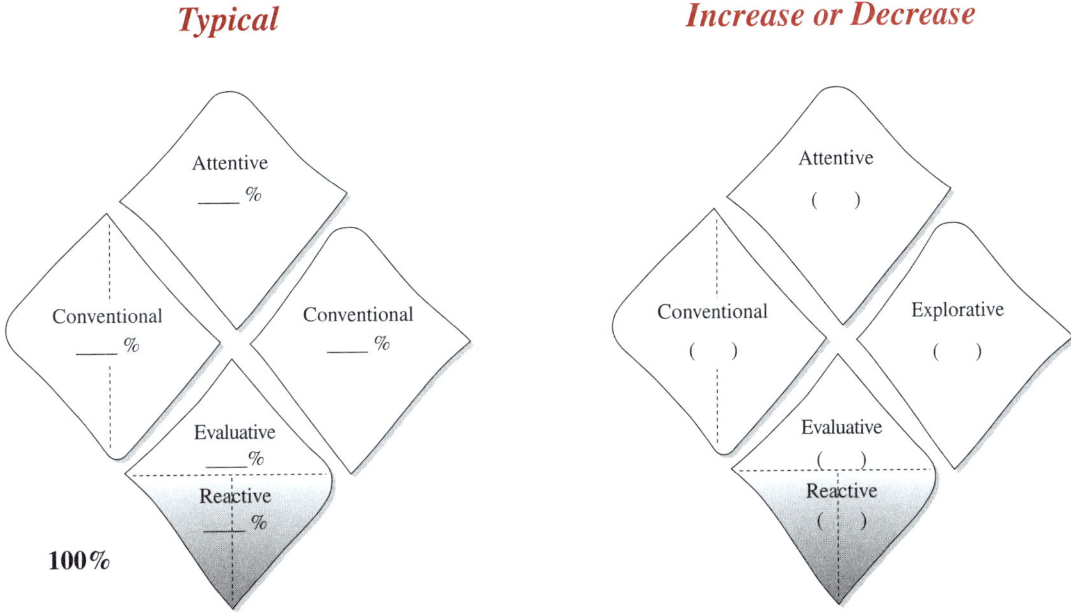

Step 3. After you and your partner both have completed these two pages, sit together, compare and discuss your perspectives.

LISTENING SKILLS ACTION PLAN

Instructions: Below is a list of the listening skills taught in this chapter. Complete the following steps:

Step 1. Without consulting your partner, mark each item twice: first with an "X" to represent your *current* use of each listening skill, and again with an "O" (circle) to represent your more-so or less-so *desired* use. If your *typical* and *desired* behaviors are the same, the "X" and "O" marks will be on the same number. If they are not the same, the marks will fall on different numbers.

When you are with your partner, how often do you:	Seldom					Often
1. Attend — look, listen, track?	1	2	3	4	5	6
2. Acknowledge his or her experience?	1	2	3	4	5	6
3. Invite more information?	1	2	3	4	5	6
4. Summarize to ensure accuracy?	1	2	3	4	5	6
5. Ask open questions?	1	2	3	4	5	6

Step 2. Choose and list one or two skills to practice between now and the next session.

Skill: _______________________________________

Skill: _______________________________________

Step 3. Compare your choices with your partner's, and talk about where and when each of you will practice using the skills.

Between Sessions

Step 4. When you notice your partner using the listening skill(s) between sessions, give him or her some positive feedback. Encourage your partner by telling how his or her use of the skill(s) makes it easier for you to tell your story accurately.

LEARNING AND APPLICATION TOOL

An additional tool, which is part of your Couple Packet, is the Listening Cycle Floor Mat. It can help you with skill practice for taking the "high road" during a conversation.

Listening Cycle Floor Mat

The Listening Cycle Floor Mat can be used at home in a couple of ways. These include:

- Prompting the listening skills as you practice them with your partner. (For specific practice on listening, set aside the Awareness Wheel floor mat.)

- Combining the listening skills practice with the talking skills practice. After you have gained more comfort with the listening skills, then with your partner, each take turns using the listening mat while the other talks about something of importance to him or her on the Awareness Wheel floor mat. (Each choose a different topical or personal issue — not a relational issue.)

BETWEEN-SESSION APPLICATIONS

Practice Listening Skills With Your Partner

In the time before the next session, invite your partner to talk about something he or she would really like you to hear. Ask him or her *not* to use the Awareness Wheel mat but just talk while you practice listening.

Use the Listening Cycle skills mat to follow your partner, to gain understanding. During this practice, do not respond or (if this involves you) do not give your own side of the story. When your partner indicates you have fully understood him or her, stop and thank your partner for helping you practice the listening skills.

Practice Listening Skills with Another Person (Not Your Partner)

With Kids:

Look for an opportunity for when a child or adolescent starts to talk or request something. Intentionally use the Attentive Listening skills to connect with him or her. Notice the impact of the conversation on the young person and on yourself.

With Someone Else (A Person at Work, Another Family Member, A Friend) in a Stressful Situation

When a situation arises, consciously use the Attentive Listening skills to understand clearly the person's perspective. Use questions wisely. Focus on following rather than on leading. Notice how your skills influence the situation.

Apologizing or Asking for Forgiveness

If you have offended your partner in some way, use your Awareness Wheel pad to reflect on your offense in preparation for a conversation with him or her. Fill out all parts of your experience.

Look for an appropriate opportunity to share your awareness about your behavior, and then apologize or ask for forgiveness.

Apply Scripture

Return to the scripture verses at the front of this chapter. Review and reflect upon them in relation to your own listening behavior. In what ways do the skills you have learned from this chapter help you apply any of the verses? According to scripture, what are some benefits from listening well?

Find a time for you and your partner to converse about your insights.

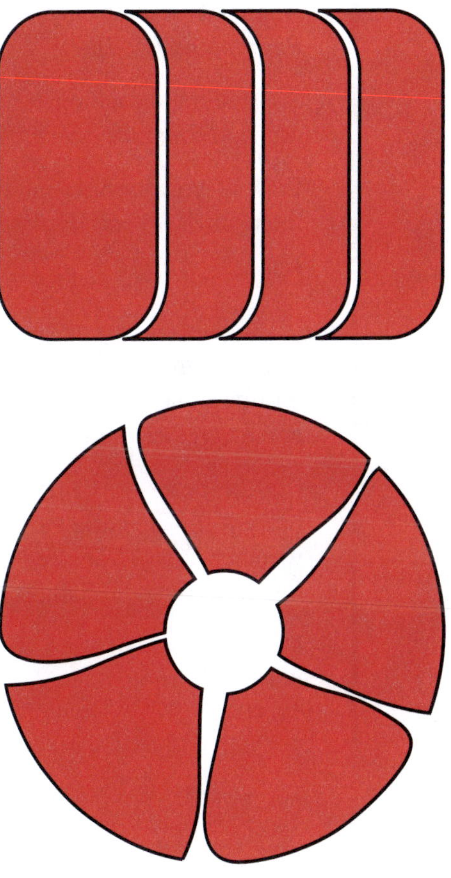

Scripture for Mapping Issues

Consider what the scriptures say for times of serious discussions and decision-making together:

Those who plan what is good find love and faithfulness. *Proverbs 14:22b*

If any of you lacks wisdom, he should ask God, who gives generously to all without finding fault, and it will be given to him. *James 1:5*

From him the whole body, joined and held together by every supporting ligament, grows and builds itself up in love, as each part does its work. *Ephesians 4:16*

And this is my prayer: that your love may abound more and more in knowledge and depth of insight, so that you may be able to discern what is best and may be pure and blameless until the day of Christ. *Philippians 1:9-10*

So encourage each other and build each other up, just as you are already doing. *I Thessalonians 5:11*

Each of you should look not only to your own interests, but also to the interests of others. *Philippians 2:4*

Let us not love with words or tongue but with actions and in truth. *I John 3:18*

I tell you that if two of you on earth agree about anything you ask for, it will be done for you by my Father in heaven. For where two or three come together in my name, there am I with them. *Matthew 19-20*

Let the peace of Christ rule in your hearts, since as members of one body you were called to peace. And be thankful. And whatever you do, whether in word or deed, do it all in the name of the Lord Jesus, giving thanks to God the Father through him. *Colossians 3:15 and 17*

May the favor of the Lord our God rest upon us; establish the work of our hands for us — yes, establish the work of our hands. *Psalm 90:17*

5

MAPPING ISSUES

A Collaborative Process for:
Making Decisions
Resolving Conflicts

Each person's experience — sensory data, thoughts, feelings, wants, and actions — of an issue is different and unique. This diversity, a dynamic in every partnership, has the potential to generate conflict, which can stimulate destructive fragmentation or creative collaboration.

Conflict can have its root in any zone of the Awareness Wheel:

- Differing perceptions of *sensory data*
- Opposing *beliefs, interpretations, expectations, values, possibilities*
- Disturbing *emotions*
- Competing *wants and interests*
- Offending *behaviors*

How you and your partner talk and listen together about your separate awarenesses of an issue influences the quality of decisions you make and your satisfaction regarding them. Likewise, the way you make decisions reveals the caring or uncaring attitudes — at least for the moment — you both hold toward one another. And, the manner in which you resolve your conflicts either strengthens or harms (emotionally or even physically) one another and your relationship.

RESOLVING ISSUES TOGETHER

Process Influences Content and Outcome

How a couple incorporates the experience and information of each partner into its process for dealing with issues is critical to the health and growth of their relationship.

- Once an issue arises, it moves by *process* — how partners talk and listen together — toward an *outcome*.

- *Process* brings out or suppresses the richness of *content*.

- Certain *processes* create better *outcomes* for both partners.

- Giving attention to improving *process* increases the likelihood of producing both richer *content* and better *outcomes* for both partners more frequently.

- Couples develop *process* patterns for dealing with issues.

- In the end, each partner feels some level of *satisfaction* (lower to higher) with the *outcome* of the issue and with the *process* they used.

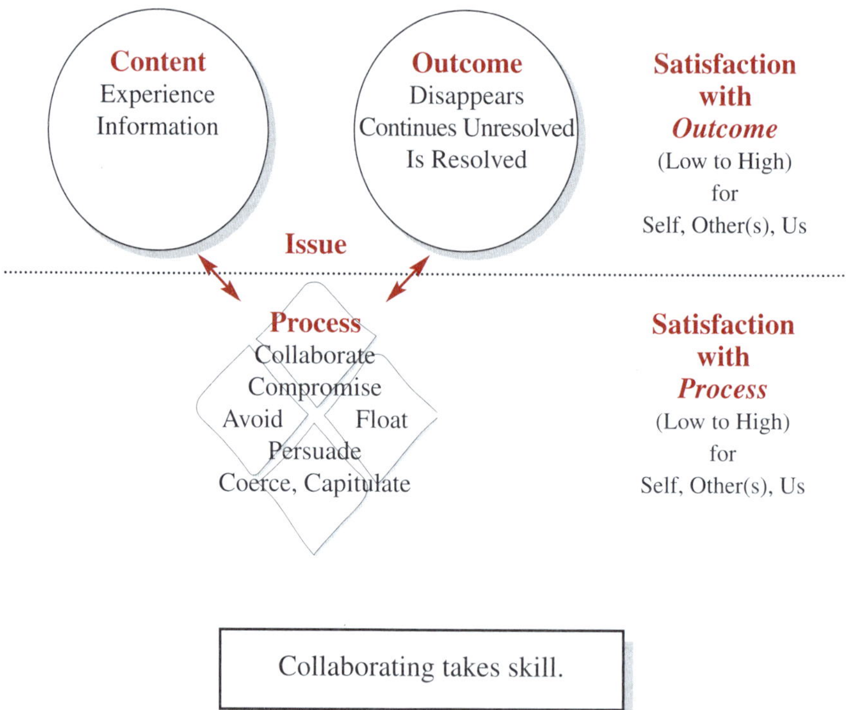

Collaborating takes skill.

ISSUE

Recall from Chapter 2 that an issue can have a primary focus, which falls into one of three categories, or that an issue can be made up of a combination of types:

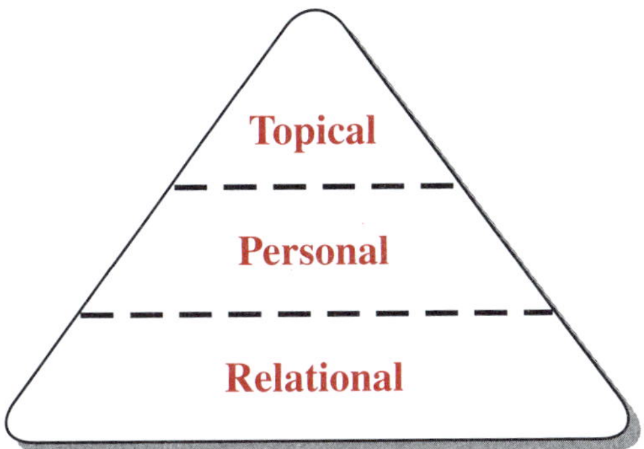

CONTENT

This is what each partner experiences, the information,about the issue.

OUTCOME

Three possible results occur, which include that the issue:

Disappears

The issue goes away by itself as time passes.

Continues Unresolved

Partners get stuck and take no action. This may include:

- Living with indecision.
- Reaching a polarized standoff (impasse).

Is Resolved

Partners take action that brings the issue to closure.

PROCESS — Style Determines Quality

When an issue arises, the talking and listening styles you and your partner use to discuss the concern establishes the *process*, which results in an *outcome* that is more or less *effective* and *satisfying* for you, your partner, and your relationship.

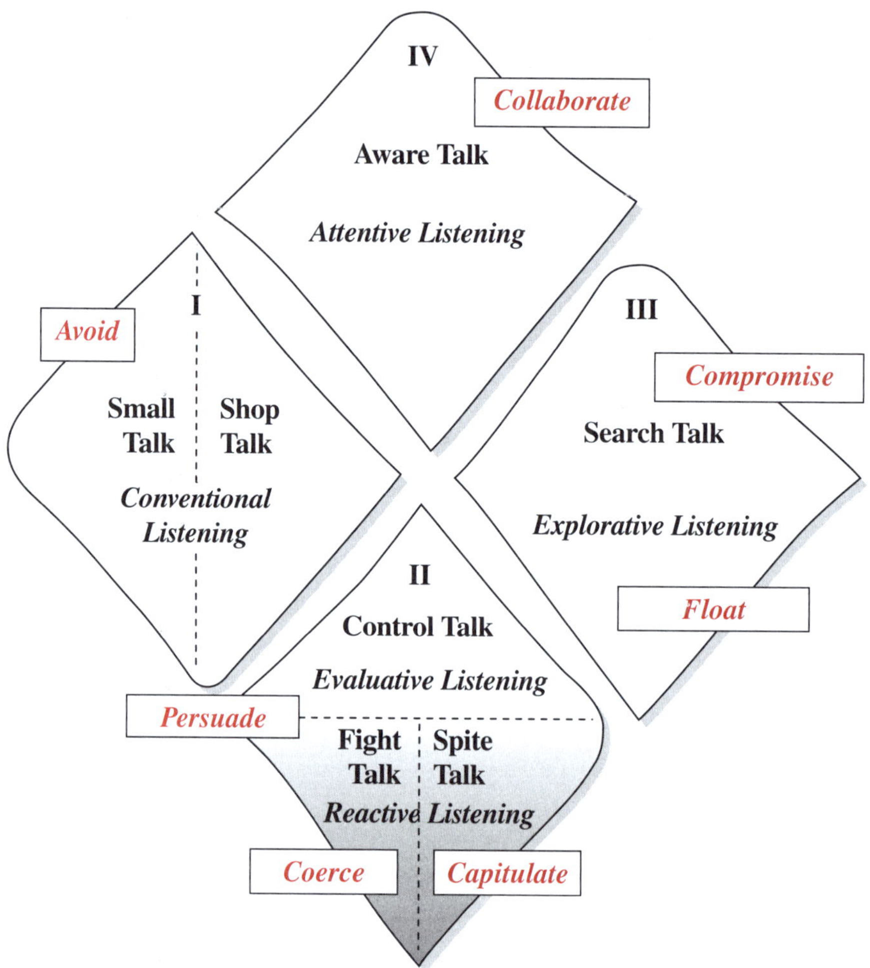

Points to Consider

- Understanding the styles and knowing the skills give you choices in how you process issues and conflicts.

- If the style you are using to resolve a conflict is not working, you can recognize its impact and shift to another style.

- Consciously shifting your Style of Communication will change the process for dealing with an issue or conflict.

AVOID

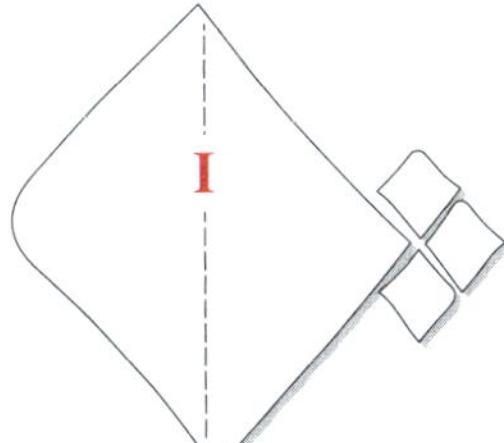

When an issue exists, you or your partner may use Small Talk, Shop Talk, and Conventional Listening to:

- Ignore it.
- Skirt around it.
- Smooth it over with chit chat.
- Joke about it.
- Change the subject.
- Claim to be too busy.
- Deny its significance.
- Leave it to chance or default.
- Refuse to discuss it.

Impact of Avoiding:

- The outcome happens by chance or default.
- Critical decisions, problems, and conflicts go unaddressed.
- Either of you (or both of you) who has something at stake in the situation is usually dissatisfied.
- Issues may disappear frequently enough for you to think that avoidance is a useful strategy.
- Sometimes avoiding may be acceptable — unless it is the only or main pattern for handling issues. (Prioritize and pick the important issues. Resolving a central issue often solves smaller issues as well. Not every issue has to be addressed individually.)

PERSUADE

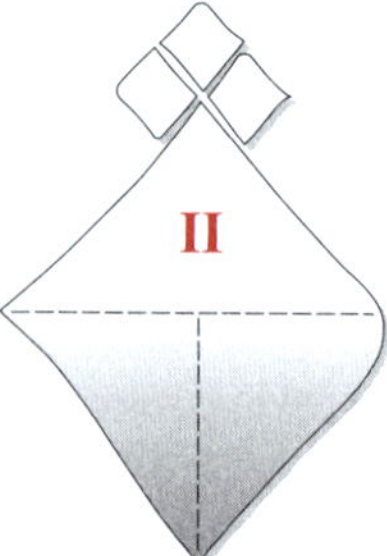

In this style, you or your partner (or both) uses Control Talk and Reactive Listening to push for agreement by:

- Making a case for a particular course of action.

- Suppressing points of view — discounting parts of the Awareness Wheel of either or both of you.

- Pressuring the other to comply.

Impact of Persuading:

- Pre-closure often occurs, bringing uninformed decisions.

- Pressure often forces "false agreements."

- When the one being persuaded is not really convinced, energy is dampened.

- Decisions become unilateral.

Impact of Coercing

If tension over the issue persists and escalates, one or both use Fight Talk:

- Arguments and fights develop. Low-road, negative emotions drive the situation.

- You struggle for power and control

- You lock up and become rigid — each fragmented and polarized in your own position — stuck in an impasse.

Impact of Capitulating

If one of you capitulates — simply complies to keep the peace or withdraws — the issue often continues unresolved under the surface. At the same time:

- Emotions about this issue and other issues blur.

- Resentment and distrust thrive. The relationship cools or is damaged.

- Underhanded, undercutting remarks and behaviors (Spite Talk) often occur.

- One partner appears to win, yet in the long run, both lose.

FLOAT

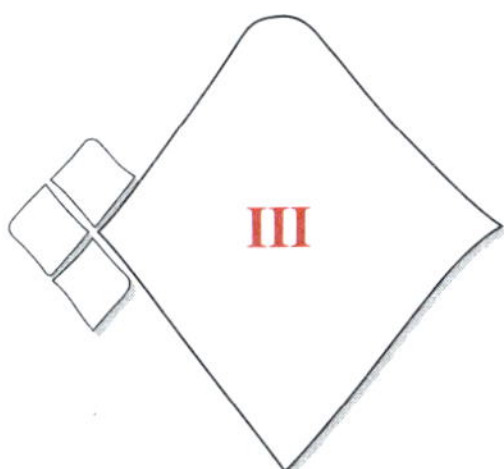

This process remains in Search Talk and Exploratory Listening for:

- Safe questions and answers.
- Speculating about causes and posing possibilities.
- Civil discussion.
- Brain-storming.
- Searching for solutions.
- Staying on the surface of an issue, without going to emotions or wants.
- Talking about, yet not, committing to take positive action.

Impact of Floating:

- No-closure happens — only talk and postponement occur.
- Little is resolved.
- Even when issues appear to be treated seriously, there is no follow-through.
- With all the discussion, partners expect something to take place, but often nothing changes.
- Indecision and lack of commitment can bring discouragement.
- While dealing with issues in this way may be safe, the cautiousness and inaction is dissatisfying.

COMPROMISE

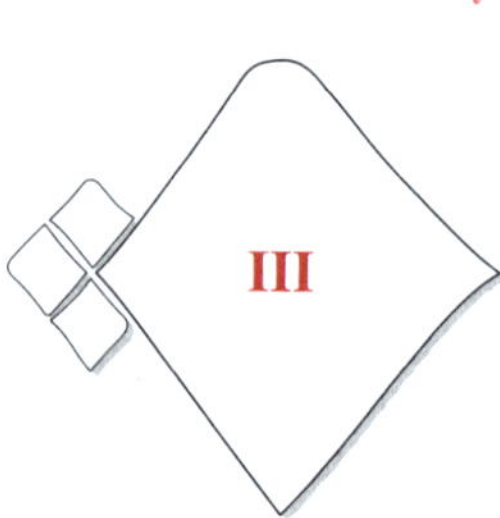

With this process, you and your partner primarily use Search Talk and Exploratory Listening to arrange a solution through trade-offs. Compromise typically falls somewhere between Search Talk and Aware Talk as each of you expresses your wants and commitment to action. You both:

- Figure out and willingly exchange concessions of differing importance to one another.

- Often operate on partial awareness, rather than complete information.

- Give something to get something.

Impact of Compromising:

- Each gains and loses something.

- Resolutions are conditional and often fragile. That is, if one of you does not keep the bargain, the other receives license to break the agreement, as well.

- Each of you tends to remember what you gave up (lost) more than what you gained (won).

- If one partner's trade becomes more valuable for some reason (after a short time) than the other's, the compromise is seen as unfair, a bad deal.

- Satisfaction is usually limited, and often leads to disappointment later.

Partners with the most good will — a caring attitude — and communication skills for processing challenging issues have the most options. Without additional knowledge and skills, compromise is the highest level of resolution most couples can achieve.

COLLABORATE

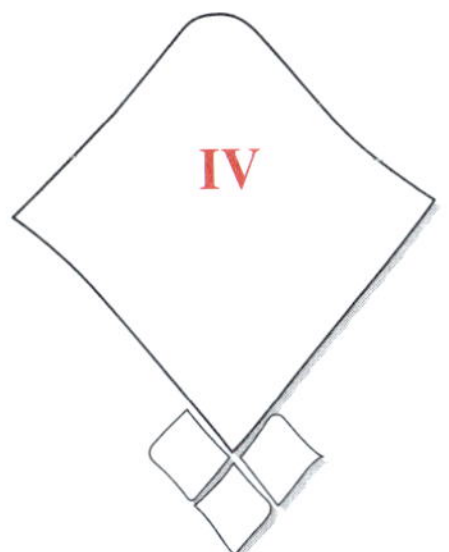

Collaboration goes beyond compromise. It draws on Aware Talk and Attentive Listening to develop understanding in order to build agreements. To do this, you both:

- Embrace common goals.

- Draw on your individual talents, experiences, and strengths.

- Disclose critical information (your full Awareness Wheels).

- Listen for understanding.

- Incorporate one another's differences.

- Bridge to each other's interests, counting both.

- Create next steps to solutions.

- Commit to follow through with congruent action.

Impact of Collaborating:

- Both you and your partner are empowered to make the most of your separate information and contributions.

- Together you invent an outcome that neither alone could have created.

- Solutions may take more time initially to achieve because they require full information and understanding.

- In the long run, time and energy are saved because fall-out from poor or partial decision-making is prevented.

- The process generates high energy and trust as you invent "best-fit" solutions.

- The process and the outcome yield the highest possible levels of creativity and satisfaction for both of you.

HOW WE DEAL WITH ISSUES AS A COUPLE

Every couple has their own ways of making decisions, solving problems, and resolving conflicts. Various process patterns result in differing levels of effectiveness and satisfaction. The diagram below shows the different *processes* and *outcomes* for dealing with issues.

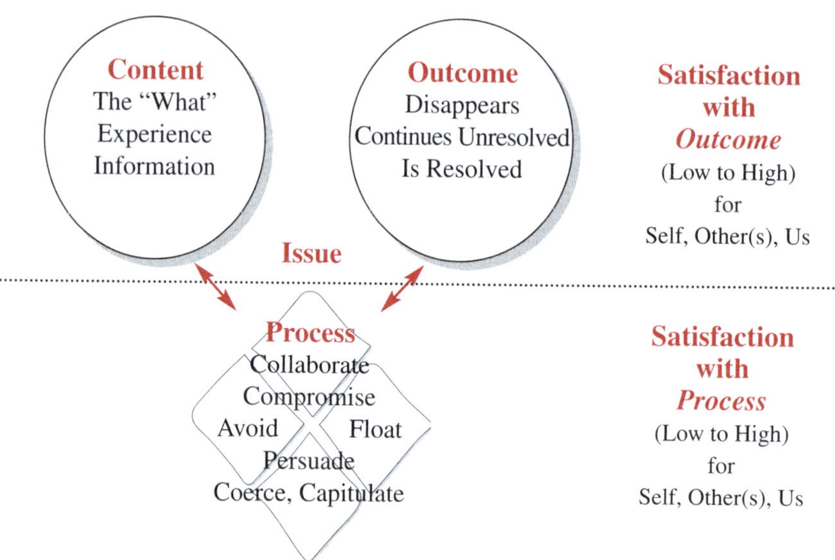

Step 1. Think about how you and your partner make decisions and resolve differences. To do this, first recall two examples of past issues. (Give a word or two to identify the issue.) Then identify the main *process* used and resulting *outcome* for each issue. Rate your *satisfaction* level with the *process* and the *outcome*. (Do not consult with your partner for this step.)

Examples:

Issue	**Process**	**Outcome**	**Satisfaction** (Low, Medium, High)	
			For Process:	*For Outcome:*

A.

B.

Step 2. Compare and discuss your processes, outcomes, and satisfaction levels with your partner. Do you see any patterns?

STEPS FOR MAPPING ISSUES

MAKING DECISIONS, SOLVING PROBLEMS, RESOLVING CONFLICTS COLLABORATIVELY

The six talking and five listening skills in COLLABORATIVE MARRIAGE SKILLS are central to making decisions, solving problems, and resolving conflicts together effectively.

When you and your partner have an important issue to discuss, you can resolve it by Mapping the Issue. This *collaborative process:*

- Covers all parts of each of your Awareness Wheels so that missing information does not come back to bite you.
- Creates alignment, optimization, and innovation.
- Helps you reach the most appropriate and satisfying outcomes.

Follow These Steps to Map-An-Issue:

- **Before Conversation**

    Step 1. Identify and Define the Issue

    Step 2. Contract to Work Through the Issue

- **During Conversation**

    Step 3. Understand the Issue Completely

    Step 4. Identify Wants for Self, Other(s), Us

    Step 5. Generate and Consider Options

    Step 6. Choose "Best-Fit" Actions

    Step 7. Test the Action Plan for "Best Fit" and Commitment

- **After Conversation**

    Step 8. Implement Future Action(s)

    Step 9. Evaluate the Outcome

WHEN TO MAP AN ISSUE

Consider Mapping the Issue When You:

- Think the issue is *important, complicated,* or *controversial.*
- Experience considerable *confusion, tension, or conflict.*
- Want *critical input* from your partner about an issue.
- Are *stuck* or *drifting.*
- Seek the *best-fit solution* for the situation.

Once you are familiar with the process, you will find it to be a good guide in any discussion through uncharted or rough territory.

STEP 1. IDENTIFY AND DEFINE THE ISSUE

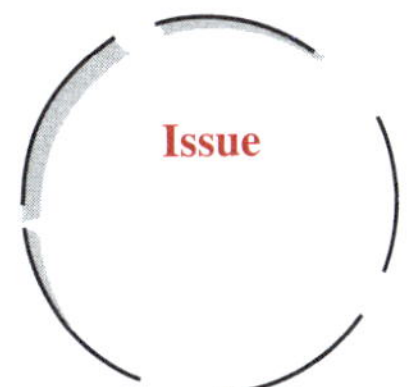

Identifying an Issue:

- An issue can arise in either partner's awareness.

- Issues typically signal a disruption in expectations — a gap between what is *anticipated* and what is actually *experienced*, between what *could be* or *should be* and what *is not*. An issue usually involves making a decision.

- The *cue* to an issue can register in any zone of your Awareness Wheel — sensing, thinking, feeling, wanting, or doing.

Defining the Issue:

- *What* is the issue?

    Topical-Task

    Personal

    Relational

- *Who* is involved?

    Self

    Partner

    Someone else (for example, an elderly parent)

When you are clear about the issue, proceed to Step 2.

STEP 2. CONTRACT TO WORK THROUGH THE ISSUE

Have you been in an exchange with your partner, wanting to talk seriously about an issue, but the discussion did not go anywhere? It is possible that you did not have a "contract" to talk about the issue.

Contracting involves:

1. *Checking both your and your partner's willingness and readiness to work through a particular issue before launching into the conversation.*
2. *Setting procedures for conducting your discussion before starting it.*

Note

- Without a good contract — a commitment to work through an issue — any discussion may be hurried, superficial, flat, or guarded, if it occurs at all.

- The more fast-paced your circumstances are or complex the issue is, the more intentional you must be about contracting as a couple.

- Contracting ensures that you are getting off to the right start.

"HUDDLING UP" — SETTING PROCEDURES

Issue	What
Procedures	Who
	Where
	When
	How

Consider these elements as you "huddle up:"

Who should be included?

- Is it just you and your partner?
- Do you want to include someone else, such as an older child?

Where will you talk?

- Choose a private place.

- Find a comfortable location.

- Limit distractions.

When will you talk?

- Consider each person's availability.

- Do not force a discussion at the wrong time or you will generate tension.

- Give time to prepare for the discussion (to fill out an Awareness Wheel if that would be helpful).

How will you talk?

Agree on a method for Mapping an Issue. Decide if you want to:

- Use the skills mats.

- Walk, sit, or ride while you converse.

- Discuss openly, using the skills.

How long will you talk?

- Set time limits for the discussion.

- Realize that conversing too long or running out of time before closure is frustrating.

Tips About Setting Procedures

- It only takes one element out of sync to dampen the process of working through an issue effectively.

- Running down this list each time you want to deal with an issue is not always necessary. Be aware, however, that an underlying informal procedural contract runs through every serious discussion.

- Nonverbals give clues about whether or not your contract to work on the issue is in effect. If you are in doubt, check it out.

- Setting procedures increases each partner's involvement and puts the the two of you in charge of your own process.

- When both partners are ready and willing — the procedures are set — a surprising amount can be accomplished, even in a limited time frame.

Sometimes Identifying the Issue and Contracting (Steps 1 and 2) are set beforehand, apart from the discussion time (Steps 3 to 7). Other times the first two steps are simply part of the Mapping-an-Issue process (up through Step 7).

TALK ABOUT TALK — Two Important Alternatives

"Check Process" (see skills mats).

"Check Process" provides a way to pause briefly in a conversation and check out what is happening (the process). This is productive any time a partner is unclear, confused, or uncomfortable with the current process.

To "Check Process," simply say, "I'd like to Check Process," meaning, "Let's pause our conversation for a moment and consider":

- "Are we on track?"

- "How are we doing listening to each other? "

- "Is it time to shift — move ahead or step back?"

- "Should we stop for now and reschedule?"

Call *"Time Out"* (see skills mats).

"Time Out" is a safety valve. It provides a way for anyone to stop a conversation. This typically occurs when:

- You or your partner are saturated or fatigued, and you become unproductive.

- Emotions are running too high, and one or both of you need time to cool.

- Additional data is needed before proceeding.

- More time is required than is currently available to resolve the issue effectively.

If one of you calls "Time Out," be sure to re-contract (check process) to discuss the issue further, when the time is right.

(Issues do not always need to be resolved at one sitting. Often, allowing time to digest what has been discussed or to gain energy brings new perspective and, at the next conversation, possibly quicker resolution.)

STEP 3. UNDERSTAND THE ISSUE COMPLETELY

The purpose of this step is to *develop complete understanding of the issue before taking action.* This prevents pre-closure — jumping quickly to solutions that do not fit.

To understand the issue, each partner answers these four sets of questions from his or her individual perspective:

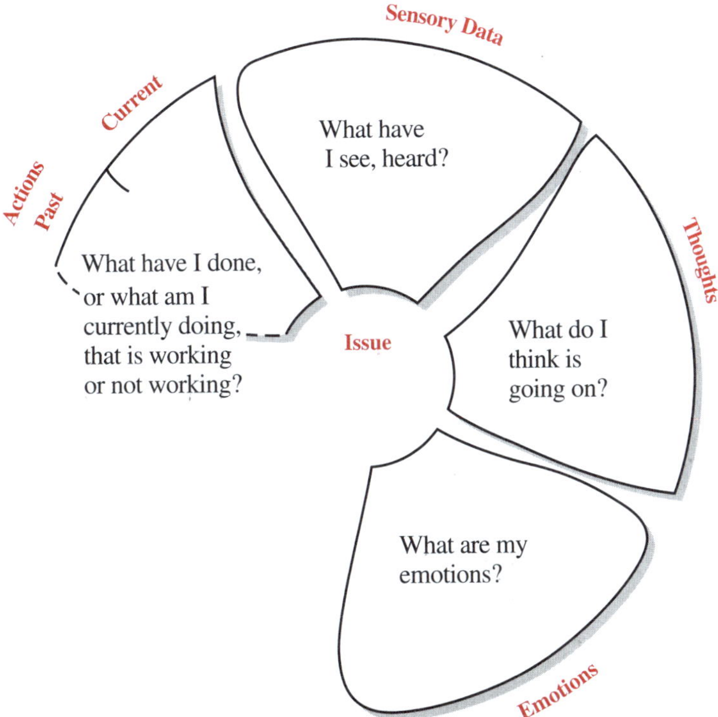

How to Understand the Issue:

- One partner at a time uses the talking skills to share his or her awareness, while the other applies the listening skills.

- Partners keep taking turns — focusing on past/current actions, data, thoughts, and emotions — until both have had a chance to share all he or she wants to say. Sometimes this step takes a while. Remember, however, that understanding is the foundation of effective and congruent future action.

Understanding as the Solution

Occasionally you will discover that it is not necessary to go beyond Step 3, because the very process of understanding the issue in itself has become the solution.

STEP 4. IDENTIFY WANTS FOR SELF, OTHER(S), US (SOU)

This step focuses on each partner's wants *for* SOU in relation to the issue.

Each asks:

- What do I want *for Self?*
- What do I want *for Other(s)* — my partner (and anyone else involved)?
- What do I want *for Us* — our relationship (for my partner and me) ?

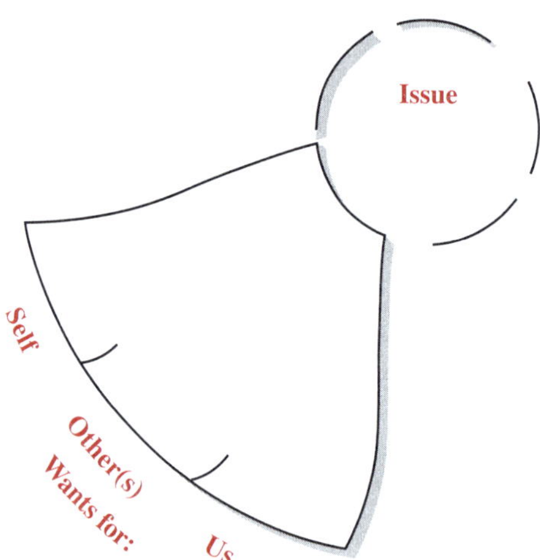

- Be careful not to confuse what you want *for* others, with what you want *from* others. (Put what you want *from* others under your wants *for* yourself.)
- Recycle stating wants for other(s) after you have heard each other's wants for self. Sometimes you do not know what you want for others until you have heard them say what they want for themselves.
- Include *don't wants* as well as *wants*.

The Key to Collaboration

In resolving conflicts, this fourth step is absolutely critical. Your success in collaborating depends on your ability to affirm and to build on the wants of your partner and of yourself.

STEP 5. GENERATE AND CONSIDER OPTIONS

For this step, you and your partner suggest possibilities about what you *could actually do to resolve the issue,* or at least take it a step ahead.

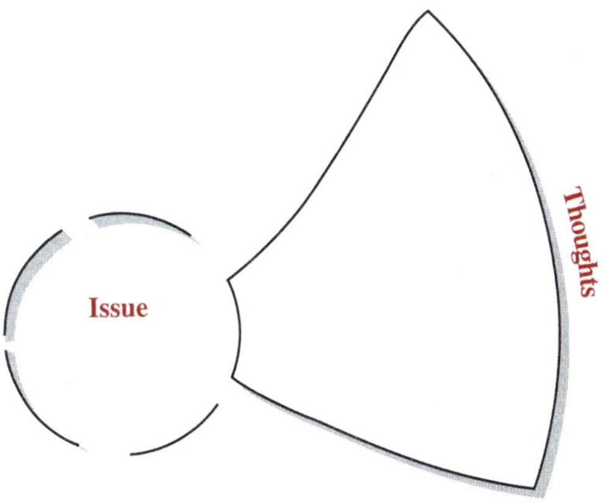

A. First, Generate Options

- Brainstorm a diverse list of small positive actions you can take as next steps, rather than try to come up with one big solution.

- Keep in view your expanded understanding of the issue (Step 3).

- Take into account wants *for* SOU (Step 4).

- Include new actions that have not been tried and past ones that have been helpful. Do not repeat what is not working.

- Do not stop to critique the options.

Sometimes it is helpful to record the options.

Options:

Option 1. ____

Option 2. ____

Option 3. ____

Option 4. ____

Option 5. ____

B. Consider the Impact of Each Potential Action on Self, Other(s), Us (SOU):

Consider the worst and best things that could happen with each action.

Draw an arrow up ↑ , down ↓ , or up and down — mixed ↑↓ to estimate the fit of each option for the SOU system. For example:

Options:	S	O	U
Option 1.	↑	↓	↓
Option 2.	↓	↑	↑
Option 3.	↑	↑	↑
Option 4.	↓	↑↓	↑
Option 5.	↑	↑	↑

In the example given above, options 3 and 5 are ones to implement.

STEP 6. CHOOSE "BEST-FIT" FUTURE ACTIONS

In this step, you and your partner select and commit to implement specific actions.

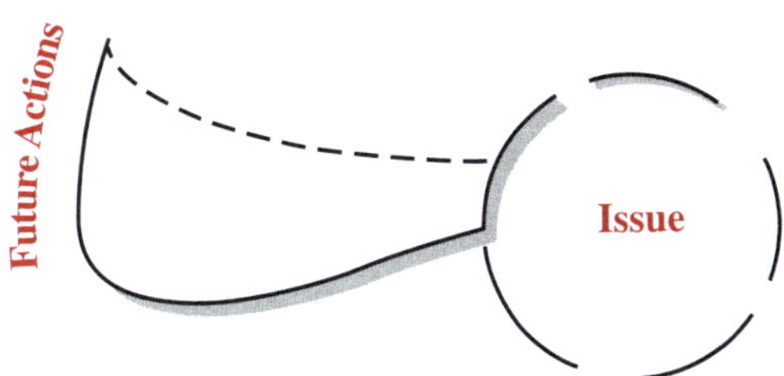

- Choose options that fit the issue/situation best. These would be actions that are the most workable and beneficial for SOU.
- Synthesize and combine options if you wish.
- Be sure the Future Action(s) are specific, positive, and achievable.
- Take small "next steps" that can leverage big change.

Make Commitments for Future Action:

- Decide who will do what by when.

Who Will Do What?	*By When?*

STEP 7. TEST THE ACTION PLAN FOR "BEST FIT" AND COMMITMENT

After you have chosen your future actions, test them by pausing for a moment and imagining yourselves actually carrying out each of the actions you have chosen to take.

- If each of you can see, hear, and experience yourself following through with each action effectively, great! Your plans fit and commitment exists.

- However, if either of you cannot imagine yourself carrying out an action, consider where in the Awareness Wheel interference occurs. Does a *thought, emotion, want,* or *action* exist that does not fit congruently and that dampens the plan? If so, talk about it. Revise the action plan to incorporate the incongruent part.

- Perhaps the incongruence signals a new issue. The zone of the Awareness Wheel in which you are stuck may be signaling a different or deeper issue that is really blocking resolution of the original issue. If time and energy are not available immediately to map and resolve the new issue, contract to deal with the new issue later.

- The incongruence may signal lack of commitment. Revisit your choice of future action.

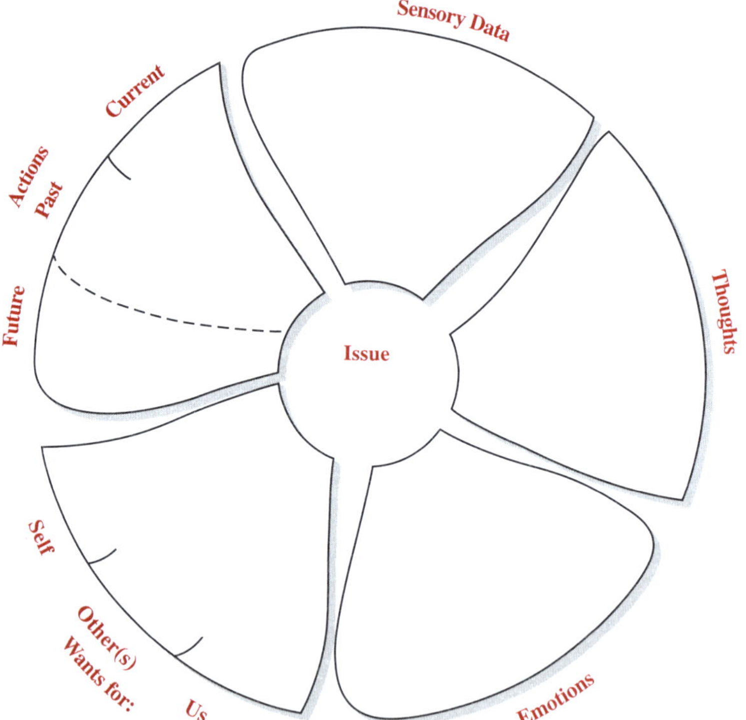

STEP 8. IMPLEMENT FUTURE ACTION(S).

This means you actually carry out the actions you have chosen, and further, that you do so within the time you have determined.

STEP 9. EVALUATE THE OUTCOME

After you have carried out your specific actions, look back to see how you have done. Ask yourselves if you have each accomplished what you committed to do, and how that has gone? If it has gone well, you may wish to celebrate in some manner.

If the outcome is not satisfactory, you may need to re-map the issue or determine if another issue emerged from this one.

MAPPING ISSUES

Instructions

Rate yourself on each of the Mapping-Issues steps below, which you practiced in the preceding exercise. Place a check mark in one of the three areas: "Needs Work," "Okay As Is," or " Did Well."

	Needs Work	Okay As Is	Did Well
■ **Before the Discussion:**			
Step 1. Identify and Define the Issue	___	___	___
Step 2. Contract to Work Through the Issue	___	___	___
■ During the Discussion			
Step 3. Understand the Issue Completely	___	___	___
Step 4. Identify Wants for SOU	___	___	___
Step 5. Generate and Consider Options	___	___	___
Step 6. Choose "Best-Fit" Action(s)	___	___	___
Step 7. Test the Action Plan for "Best Fit" and Commitment	___	___	___
■ After Discussion (Rate yourself later, after doing the steps.)			
Step 8. Implement Future Action(s)	___	___	___
Step 9. Evaluate the Outcome	___	___	___

- As partners, compare your ratings (for Steps 1 - 7).
- Choose steps to improve.

Action Plan

- During the next week, select an issue and map the issue with your partner using both skills mats. Be sure to attend to the steps you have chosen to improve. Remember to consider and build in wants for each other and your relationship.

Once you have completed the COUPLE COMMUNICATION I program, plan something special to celebrate your relationship.

Then, do the following activities to continue your growth:

- Retake ThriveSphere (by contacting your instructor).
- Review your results and compare them with the first time you took ThriveSphere.

    Notice areas of gain.

    Identify any areas for continued development.

- Select an issue from your ThriveSphere-Chart, or use another concern, to map an issue together. Use your Awareness Wheel and Listening Cycle floor skills mats to guide you in your conversation.
- Continue to use the talking and listening skills and other tools to enrich your day-to-day conversations, and map issues as they arise.
- Set a date, within a year from your having taken ThriveSphere the first time, to retake ThriveSphere for a picture of your continued growth.
- Ask your instructor about taking COUPLE COMMUNICATION II.

Choose a Scripture Verse

Review the scripture verses at the beginning of Chapter 5, and with your partner, select a verse that has special meaning for your marriage. Commit the verse to memory.

M. Bear, B. Connors, and M. Paradiso, *Neuroscience: Exploring the Brain*, 2nd Edition, (Baltimore and Philadelphia: Lippincott Williams & Wilkins, 2001).

L. Cozolino, *The Neuroscience of Human Relationships: Attachment and the Developing Social Brain*, (New York and London: W.W. Norton & Company, 2006).

D. Goleman, *Social Intelligence: The New Science of Human Relationships*, (New York: Bantam Dell/Random House, 2006).

P. Lawson, and R. Lindstrom, *Being Spherical: Reshaping Our Lives and Our World for the 21st Century*, (Evergreen, CO: Sphericity Press, 2004).

J. LeDoux, *The Emotional Brain: The Mysterious Underpinnings of Emotional Life*, (New York: Simon & Schuster, 1996).

D. Siegel, *The Developing Mind: Toward a Neurobiology of Interpersonal Experience*, (New York: Guilford Publications, 1999).

Stanley, S. *The Power of Commitment: A Guide to Active, Lifelong Love*, (San Francisco: Jossey-Bass, 2005).

For a summary of research on COUPLE COMMUNICATION, see the website www.couplecommunication.com

COUPLE COMMUNICATION II

If you have benefited from the COUPLE COMMUNICATION I program, we welcome you to participate in the COUPLE COMMUNICATION II program, as well.

COUPLE COMMUNICATION II reinforces the 11 communication skills for building a "collaborative operating system" to enrich your conversations and decision-making process. The advanced program helps you to manage your own anger effectively and guides you to respond to your partner's anger skillfully. The program also helps you bring your values, desires, and plans into alignment with one another. Ask your instructor for details or check the website: www.couplecommunication.com.

CORE COMMUNICATION: SKILLS AND PROCESSES

The CORE COMMUNICATION program teaches the same frameworks, skills, and processes as the COUPLE COMMUNICATION program, however, instead of focusing on couples, it is directed to individuals.

Besides the content of the five chapters in this *Collaborative Marriage Skills* workbook, CORE contains additional material for helping individuals to communicate effectively under pressure and to create communication strategies for various personal and professional situations. It also gives strategies for responding to the communication styles of Fight Talk and Spite Talk. For more information, visit www.comskills.com.

BUSINESS PROGRAMS

The collaborative maps, skills and processes taught in COUPLE COMMUNICATION are available for businesses.

COLLABORATIVE TEAM SKILLS

As teams solve problems, they make critical decisions regularly. When members run into conflict, the way they resolve or lock up over their differences impacts their team and business development. The COLLABORATIVE TEAM SKILLS system provides tools to enhance the competence of team members and the team collectively in all these processes — solving problems, making decisions, and resolving conflicts — resulting in improved performance.

THE I-SKILLSZONE SYSTEM

Companies spend large sums of money on hardware and software to create a "common operating system" that connects all of their information technology. When the I-SKILLSZONE SYSTEM becomes part of a company's culture, it provides a common collaborative "human operating system" for conducting productive conversations and building collaborative relationships up, down, and across the organization. Profitability increases when players are on the same page — sharing a common language for discovering, discussing, resolving, and aligning information — that supports business development.

Companies incorporate the I-SKILLSZONE SYSTEM for:

- Communication and Conflict Resolution Skills Training
- Leadership Development
- Performance Improvement Initiatives
- Change Management Process
- Team Building (The I-SKILLSZONE SYSTEM is more comprehensive than, and may be substituted for, COLLABORATIVE TEAM SKILLS.)

For more information on bringing COLLABORATIVE TEAM SKILLS or I-SKILLSZONE SYSTEM into your company, visit: www.I-SkillsZone.com.

Sherod Miller, Ph.D., is CEO of Interpersonal Communication Programs, Inc. (ICP), a publishing and training company headquartered in Evergreen, Colorado. He is a master trainer, specializing in teaching others how to teach the ICP communication systems.

Phyllis A. Miller, Ph.D., is President of Interpersonal Communication Programs, Inc., where she serves as editor and directs instructor certification of ICP programs. Phyllis and Sherod enjoy a collaborative marriage and business partnership together.

Elam Nunnally, Ph.D., is a Professor Emeritus at the University of Wisconsin-Milwaukee. He is also a marriage and family therapist, and clinical social worker. He is one of the originators of solution-focused therapy, which he teaches in Wisconsin and Scandinavia.

Daniel B. Wackman, Ph.D., is a Professor in the School of Journalism and Mass Communication at the University of Minnesota. Much of his research has focused on family processes and child development. He also serves as a consultant to business, nonprofit organizations, and government agencies. His most recent book is *Managing Media Organizations: Effective Leadership of the Media*.